Celtic
Saints
of Wales

CELTIC SAINTS OF WALES

ELIZABETH REES

FONTHILL

Front cover illustration: St Luke, from the Lichfield Gospels

Back cover illustration: Aberdaron church, Gwynedd

Fonthill Media Limited
Fonthill Media LLC
www.fonthillmedia.com
office@fonthillmedia.com

First published in the United Kingdom 2015

British Library Cataloguing in Publication Data:
A catalogue record for this book is available from the British Library

Typeset in 10pt on 13pt Minion Pro
Printed and bound in Great Britain by CPI Group (UK) Ltd, Croydon, CR0 4YY

Contents

Preface

Before Christianity reached Ireland, there were probably Christians in Wales who arrived with the Roman army and administration. Inscriptions suggest that they were educated people, who spoke Latin rather than Welsh. In the fifth and sixth centuries, Christians travelled from Gaul to Wales, where gravestones are inscribed in a style found in Gaul.

By this time, monasteries were well established in Gaul, and immigrants brought with them an experience of monastic life. By the early sixth century there were a number of Welsh communities, and the monastic tradition spread rapidly. As in Ireland, early Welsh monasteries included both monks and non-monastic priests; they were presided over by an abbot, who was often a bishop. He might be married, and leadership could be handed down through the family.

This book summarises what we know about these early Welsh Christians, drawing on archaeology, early inscriptions, and also upon Lives of these men and women written by later monks. However, these biographies often contain few historical facts. The book is illustrated by photographs which I have taken at the sites where the Welsh saints lived and worked.

I am not primarily a scholar; I write as a single, vowed woman, out of my experience of religious life. This has encouraged me to explore the values and ideals of earlier monks and nuns. I am grateful to Professor Jonathan Wooding and Dr Karen Jankulak for their generous help over the years, and to my sister, Frances Jones, for her help with reproducing the illustrations. Any errors are my own.

Elizabeth Rees

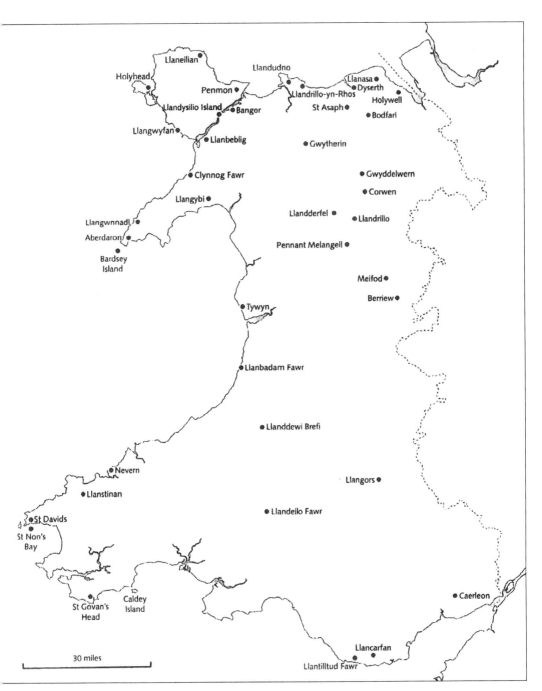

Wales: chief sites described in the text.

PART I
SAINTS OF SOUTH WALES

The Search for Holiness

The Arrival of Christianity

In the second and third centuries, there were Christians in Britain who had been converted and baptised, often secretly, in other Roman provinces, in Gaul, or in places further to the east. Christian soldiers also arrived in Britain with the Roman army. Christianity was a permitted religion from AD 260, but Christians worshipped one God and acknowledged neither the gods of Rome nor the deified emperors. This ran contrary to Roman thought and belief, and led to periodic persecutions. The British monk Gildas (d. *c.* 570), tells us of martyrs: Alban in Verulamium (St Albans), and Aaron and Julius, citizens of Urbs Legionum, which was probably Caerleon in south-east Wales.[1]

Constantine was proclaimed emperor in 306; a convert himself, he was the first emperor to grant liberty of conscience to Christians. In 313 the Edict of Milan announced the restoration of confiscated churches and freedom of worship. The remains of Christian cemeteries and churches indicate that by the fourth century, Christians had spread through many areas of England and Wales, into town and countryside.

In the Roman Empire, Christianity was centred on urban life; pastoral care was organised by bishops who lived in towns. British bishops are first recorded in attendance at the Council of Arles in 314. They headed communities in the capitals of the four Roman provinces of fourth-century Britain: London, York, Lincoln, and Cirencester. Bishops were soon found in some twenty other British towns, as far north as Carlisle and probably as far as Exeter, in the south-west, and Carmarthen, in south Wales.

Gildas

From the fifth century onwards, Christians set up memorial stones to their dead, many of which still survive. However, when the Romans departed from Britain in AD 410, the economy began to collapse and towns gradually fell into ruin. We know little about British Christianity immediately after the Romans withdrew, apart from what we find in the work entitled *On the Ruin and Conquest of Britain* (*De Excidio et Conquestu Britanniae*) by

Gildas. This is our only significant source for the history of fifth- and sixth-century Britain written by a near contemporary.

Gildas was not writing a history book; his intention was to preach to the rulers of his time, as the Old Testament prophets had done. His book takes the form of a lengthy sermon condemning the behaviour of both secular and religious leaders, whom he blames for the dire state of the nation. He describes its rulers by using the allegory of the powerful and destructive beasts portrayed by the prophet Daniel (Dan. 3. 3–7) in the Old Testament and the Book of Revelation (Rev. 13. 1–3) at the end of the New Testament.

He hints at a long tradition of established Christianity, describing a Church that is familiar to us in some ways, and yet strange in others. It was organised on a territorial basis, although parishes did not yet exist. Gildas frequently mentions bishops, presbyters, deacons and clerics in lesser orders. He describes the bishops as skilfully versed in the complexities of worldly affairs; they are men of social and political standing. The clergy have flocks (*greges*) who gather in churches (*domus ecclesiae*) to celebrate the Eucharist; celibacy is not required of clerics. Gildas speaks of unbelievers (*increduli*) who require missionaries to preach to them. The Church is oriented towards Rome in its faith and worship.

Gildas describes ambitious clerics who travel to Gaul in order to be consecrated as bishops and then proudly return. He depicts the Church during the last years of the declining Roman Empire. In his Penitential (or manual of punishments for crimes), Gildas uses Roman weights and measures, and he employs many other Roman terms in 'The Ruin of Britain'. Gildas quotes from Jerome's new Vulgate translation of the Bible, but he prefers the Old Latin version, and draws on an early translation of the Book of Job used in Roman times.[2] Gildas thus describes a church in south Britain which was built on Roman foundations.

Monasteries were a new development, and were to grow in significance in the following centuries. Gildas tells us that the Welsh King Maelgwyn spent some time in one, and describes its rules, its emphasis on teaching scripture to the young, and the practice of chanting psalms. He describes bishops who continue to govern the Church, while perhaps living in the new monastic communities. Gildas is very critical of his contemporaries; he is horrified that the Cornish King Constantine committed sacrilege by murdering royal youths at a monastery, and he condemns another ruler for abandoning his plan of becoming a monk. Gildas considers that society is full of wicked men, but he describes them as being wicked in a Christian context.[3]

Martin of Tours

Gildas hints at the origin of monastic life in Britain, relating how Christians went into solitude in search of God. After he describes the martyrdom of Alban, Julius, and Aaron, he continues: 'The survivors hid in woods, desert places and secret caves, looking towards God'.[4] This form of life had already begun in Gaul, where Bishop Martin of Tours (*c.* 316–97) established a monastery at Marmoutier that became a model for successive generations of monks and nuns throughout Europe. Using language similar to that of Gildas a century later, Martin's friend and biographer Sulpicius Severus describes Marmoutier's isolation:

> The place was so secluded and remote that it had all the solitude of the desert. On one side it was walled in by the rock face of a high mountain, and the level ground that remained was enclosed by a gentle bend of the River Loire. There was only one approach to it, and that a very narrow one.[5]

There were, of course, no deserts in Gaul, but the Latin word *desertum* used by Severus means 'an empty space'. In his account of Martin's monastery, Sulpicius was alluding to the tradition of the Desert Mothers and Fathers of the Near East; these men and women left the cities in search of an 'empty place' in which to pray. The monks and nuns of the eastern deserts often chose locations that were remote, but not too far from towns; they could therefore exercise hospitality and help their urban neighbours in practical ways. We read in the *Lives of the Desert Fathers*: 'There is no town or village in Egypt … which is not surrounded by hermitages as if by walls'.[6]

The monk Copres taught peasants how to make their land more fertile; John of Lycopolis predicted the rise and fall of the Nile and the annual yield of the crops, which enabled farmers to work more wisely. Serapion sent wheat and clothing to the poor in Alexandria, since those in his neighbourhood already had sufficient. The *Historia Monachorum* describes monks dealing with farmers, Romans, merchants and civil servants in towns and villages.[7] The Greek name *monachos*, or monk, means 'one who is alone', but the earliest surviving reference to a monk is in a fourth-century Greek papyrus found in Egypt, which records a village squabble in which one of the two witnesses is a *monachos*.

In Gaul, Martin's monastery was in an isolated spot, yet only 2 miles from Tours, so the bishop was able to commute between his monastic retreat and his episcopal duties in the town. The location of Marmoutier influenced early British monks in their choice of sites. Rivers were major routes, and many British and Irish monasteries are found beside a river and near a chieftain's settlement.

Sulpicius Severus describes the monks at Martin's monastery as men of prayer, who shared all they had. Younger men, with good eyesight perhaps, copied sacred texts, but unnecessary work was avoided:

> No one possessed anything of his own; everything was put into the common stock. The buying and selling which is customary with most hermits was forbidden to them. No craft was practised there except that of copyist, and that was assigned to younger men. The older ones were left free for prayer. Rarely did anyone of them go outside their cell, except when they assembled at the place of prayer. They all took their food together, after the hour of fasting was past. No one drank wine, except when illness compelled them to do so.[8]

The Life of Martin was widely distributed and became a popular text in the early British Church, providing a model of holy living.

The Call to Holiness

If you felt a call to holiness, how could you follow it? The safest way was to find another person or group who were already pursuing such a call. With them, you could learn to model your life on holy people in the scriptures—the prophet Elijah in the Old Testament and John the Baptist in the gospels, each of whom became 'father' to a community of disciples.[9] You could also take as models the Desert Mothers and Fathers who had been visited by western monks such as Cassian from Gaul, and by nuns such as Egeria from north-west Spain, both of whom visited the Near East in the 380s. Throughout medieval times, St Antony, Paul the Hermit, Macarius, and other desert-dwellers inspired western Christians to pursue holiness.

What did it mean to be a monk or nun in the early Welsh Church? There was a wide variety of contrasting lifestyles, each of which was an expression of the monastic ideal. You might be a solitary or live in community. You might remain in your tribal territory, or perhaps feel called to leave it as a pilgrim for Christ. Your life could be extremely austere, or more balanced and moderate. You might devote much time to study, as in the monastery at Llanbadarn Fawr (see Chapter 3) or spend most of your day in hard agricultural labour, as in St David's monastery (see Chapter 2). There was interplay between these various extremes: Bishop Samson, whose life will be explored in Chapter 4, left his community in order to find solitude with a few close friends, and later set out with them as a pilgrim for the love of God.

Hermits

During the second half of the fifth century, a soldier named Sidonius Apollinarus (*c.* 430–80) became bishop of Clermont-Ferrand in Gaul. He wrote poems and letters, and in a poem that he wrote to Faustus of Riez (461–93) he describes the different locations where hermits live—in the African desert, in marshes (such as those with which he was familiar around the mouth of the River Loire), in caves, or on Alpine mountain slopes. Faustus may have been born in Britain; he was abbot of the monastery of Lérins in southern Gaul, and was some thirty years younger than Sidonius.

In the poem, Sidonius recalls the great models of sainthood from which the young abbot can take encouragement. Faustus had a reputation on account of his austerity, and Sidonius does not conceal his admiration for young Faustus. He writes:

Whether you stay, roughly clad, in the inhospitable wilderness [in Latin: *tesqua*] beside the sun-baked Syrtes [a shallow sea off the north African coast], or whether you choose a green, slimy marsh, or clefts of rock, with deep sunless caves in perpetual gloom, or if you choose the Alps, whose steep mountain ranges stretch far into the distance, yet all these will tremble before you, great hermit, as you snatch a brief sleep on the chilly ground, and with all their cold they can never overcome the warm glow that Christ has put in your heart.

> For this is the way that you are urged to live by the Prophet Elijah and John the Baptist, by the two great Abbots Macarius ... Again, you are called to this by Antony [of Egypt], who wore nothing but a tunic made of palm leaves from the kind hand of [God] his Master.[10]

Sidonius uses the Latin word *tesqua* to describe these different kinds of wilderness. This word often appears in pre-Christian literature, but was rarely used by Christians. The only other time that *tesqua* appears in a Christian context is a century later, when St Isidore of Seville (*c*. 560–636) explains its meaning in his *Etymologies*: '*Tesqua* is called by some a hut and by others a steep and hard place'.[11] This well describes a hermit's cell in an inhospitable landscape.

Ditoc's Little Desert

The word *tesqua* occurs once in Wales (in its diminutive form *tesquitus*, meaning 'a little desert'), on a pillar stone at Llanllŷr, 5 miles north of Lampeter in Ceredigion. The pillar, shown overleaf, dates from between the seventh and the ninth century, and the word *tesquitus* is used to describe the marshy desert dwelling of a hermit named Ditoc, in the broad valley of the River Aeron. The pillar stands in the grounds of Llanllŷr House; Llanllŷr means 'church site of Llŷr', and perhaps refers to a local monk or nun.

Ditoc's small waste plot lay at the end of a causeway across the marsh, in the hamlet of Talsarn. Place names offer us vital clues about early settlements, and in this case, *sarn* denotes an early paved road, while *tal* means 'the end of the road'. We can perhaps imagine Ditoc living on a small patch raised above the surrounding bog. A hermit needs a supply of fresh water, and there is a spring at the site whose water is so abundant and pure that today it is bottled and sold globally by the Llanllŷr Water Company.

The roughly-shaped pillar is of local Llandovery Silurian stone, and is likely to have been carved at the site. Set beneath a ringed cross, the Latin inscription is one of the few surviving examples of a *contractus*, or text used as a charter. Although the text is short, only one or two early British inscriptions contain such a wealth of detail. The stone commemorates Ditoc, who by now had probably died, and describes how the plot's owner, Aon, gifts the land to the monastery of an Irish saint, Modomnóc, who was a disciple of David. Much later Modomnóc, whose name means 'My little Dovnan', will be described in glowing terms by David's eleventh-century biographer, Rhygyfarch.[12]

The inscription is carved in round half-uncials, neatly picked. It reads downwards: 'TESQUITUS DITOC/MADOMNUACO/AON FILIUS ASA/ITGEN DEDIT', or 'The small hermitage of Ditoc [which] Aon, son of Asa Itgen gave to [Saint] Modomnóc'. The names on the monument are Irish, which might have been expected in the Irish-speaking kingdom of Dyfed, south of the River Teifi, but is less common north of the Teifi, in Ceredigion; this suggests that Ditoc was an Irish hermit living in exile outside Pembrokeshire. Sadly, the second half of the memorial slab was broken up and recycled as building stone before its value was recognised.

Inscribed cross, Llanllŷr, Ceredigion.

A community of Cistercian nuns was founded at Llanllŷr in around 1180 from Strata Florida Abbey, 15 miles to the north-east, by the Lord Rhys, ruler of Deheubarth (or south Wales). There were surprisingly few convents in Wales; in later medieval times, there were only three Welsh religious houses of women, compared with 150 in England, sixty-four in Ireland, and fifteen in Scotland. In or around 1377 there were four nuns and an abbess at Llanllugan in Powys, perhaps thirteen at Usk in Gwent, and sixteen nuns at Llanllŷr, which was therefore the largest women's community in Wales at that time. By comparison, there were some 2,000 nuns in English convents at the dissolution of the monasteries.[13]

Beside the memorial stone at Llanllŷr, there is a medieval culvert (or underground water channel). The monastic fishponds survive, but the convent was destroyed in 1537 at the dissolution of the monasteries, and a Tudor mansion was built from its remains. In 2014 the convent and its cemetery were excavated: the convent was well-built, and fragments of glazed floor tiles indicated that it was finely decorated. The nuns farmed sheep and cattle and owned mills and orchards.[14]

Christians as Bees

While monks like Ditoc were hermits, others lived in community. Early Jewish Christians likened communities of Christians to an ordered honeycomb of bees, feeding together on the sweetness of God's word and making honey for others around them to enjoy.[15] Early monks, too, saw themselves as bees in a hive, gathering the nectar of God's love and making it into honey for themselves and others to eat, under the leadership of a wise and experienced queen bee, their abbot. They gathered the nectar of God's word by chanting the psalms and listening to the scriptures, transforming what they heard into honey which nourished others and brought them healing and enjoyment.

Each week, they chanted in the psalms:

The decrees of the Lord are truth …
and sweeter are they than honey
that drips from the comb (Ps. 18. 10, 11).[16]

And from the longest psalm, which was a favourite with Celtic monks:

Your promise is sweeter to my taste
than honey in the mouth (Ps. 118. 103).

Although early monks thought of God's word as honey that they must eat and digest, sometimes this could be painful. They recalled God's command to the Old Testament prophet Ezekiel, who is depicted as swallowing a scroll of prophetic warnings, on which was written 'lamentations, wailings, moanings': 'Son of man, eat what is given to you, then go and speak to the House of Israel … I ate it, and it tasted sweet as honey' (Ezk. 2. 8 - 3. 3). Each of the prophets discovered that God's message could be bittersweet.

Like good monks, bees also worked tirelessly; they collaborated with monks by producing wax for candles to use in worship. On Easter night, the deacon chanted the Exultet, an ancient song in praise of the paschal candle, whose flame represented the light of the risen Christ. In the Exultet, which dates from between the fifth and the seventh century, he praises the bees which made the wax for the Easter candle:

A solemn offering, the work of bees and of your servants' hands …
for it is fed by melting wax drawn out by the mother bees
to build a torch so precious.

Although bees are busy in their hive, they come out and buzz around a stranger. At the end of the fourth century, an Italian monk—Rufinus of Aquileia—recalled his stay with the desert monks in Egypt:

When we came near, they realised that foreign monks were approaching, and at once they swarmed out of their cells like bees. They joyfully hurried to meet us.[17]

Strength with Sweetness

In the Old Testament, Samson was an ancient warrior leader born to a barren woman; his birth was announced by an angel (Judges 13. 2–7), like that of John the Baptist, the

Memorial to Dallus Dumelus, 'Fort of honey', Llanddewi Brefi, Ceredigion.

forerunner of Jesus. Samson 'began to rescue Israel' and was considered as a model for monks, although his violent exploits might cause consternation today. While on campaign with his followers, he came across a colony of bees making honey inside the carcass of a young lion that he had killed earlier. Pondering this sight, he observed: 'Out of the strong came forth sweetness' (Judges 14. 14).

Early monks understood this as a description of their calling: a monk was a young lion with honey in his heart, or, more precisely, a monk was a strong young man whose body was dead to this world's pleasures, while his heart was a honeycomb dripping with love. A monk learned how to become strong in virtue and sweet in manner, combining fortitude with kindness. As we shall see in Chapter 4, a sixth-century monk who was also named Samson is depicted in similar terms—he is presented as a young man austerely detached from this world, yet full of the honey of God's love.

Among the early memorial stones to abbots of St David's monastery at Llanddewi Brefi, in Ceredigion, a seventh-century stone commemorates a monk named Dallus Dumelus. Dallus means '[God's] portion', or 'an offering to God', while Dumelus is an Irish name derived from *dun* ('fort') and *mel* ('honey'), meaning something like 'Fort of honey'. Like the two Samsons, Dumelus was evidently strong in spirit, yet with sweetness of heart.

St David Blesses Bees

The Irish *Martyrology of Óengus*, which was written in the early 800s at Tallaght, near Dublin, describes an incident in which St David blessed a hive of bees from his monastery. Their beekeeper was one of David's Irish disciples, Modomnóc, whom we have already met at Llanllŷr. When Modomnóc set sail for Ireland, his bees followed him: 'In a little boat, from the east, over the pure-coloured sea, my Domnóc brought—vigorous cry!—the gifted race of Ireland's bees'.[18] It is possible that 'vigorous cry!' means 'buzz!', a sound which would indeed be experienced as vigorous in a silent monastery; in early poetry, the choice of adjective (here, the unexpected word 'vigorous') was often dictated by the fact that syllables had to be scanned into poetic lines of fixed length.[19]

In the late eleventh century, David's biographer, Rhygyfarch, elaborates the story of Modomnóc's bees:

> Boarding a ship, a large swarm of bees followed [Modomnóc] and settled with him in the prow of the ship where he sat. For he, attending the bee hives in addition to the rest of the work of the community, gave attention to the bee hives in order to nourish the swarms of young bees, so that he might provide the pleasure of some more agreeable food for the needy.[20]

Three times Modomnóc returned to the monastery with the bees, until finally David blessed the swarm, saying 'May the land to which you are hurrying be abundant with your offspring; may your progeny never be lacking in it'. This, we are told, is how bees came to Ireland.

St Govan's Chapel

Apart from inscribed crosses and other memorial stones, there are almost no early remains at Welsh monastic sites; but there are some hermitages built on early foundations in dramatic locations. The cliffs around the Welsh coast provided caves which offered a hermit shelter, with a fine view over the sea and the prospect of fishing and collecting seabirds' eggs for food. The Christian tradition of living in caves dates back to the time of the Desert Mothers and Fathers of the Near East. They took literally the words of the Letter to the Hebrews in the New Testament, which describe God's holy ones living in the same manner: 'They were too good for the world and they went out to live in deserts and mountains, and in caves and ravines' (Heb. 11. 38).

One of the most dramatic hermitages in Wales is St Govan's chapel in Pembrokeshire, where a cleft in the rock was extended to create a chapel that clung to the cliffs. An additional attraction for an early hermit was a freshwater spring at the foot of the cliffs, over which a well house was later built; there was also a spring welling up in the chapel.

St Govan's chapel is a mile south of Bosherston and 7 miles south of Pembroke, on the south coast. To find the chapel, drive past St Govan's Inn, Bosherston. Continue along the Range Road to St Govan's, and park at the top of the cliffs. The chapel is soon visible down the cliff path. The tiny oratory is wedged in a narrow cleft halfway down the cliff, and is reached by fifty-two steps. It may date from the eleventh century, but its foundations are probably earlier.

Above left: St Govan's chapel, St Govan's Head, Pembrokeshire.

Above right: St Govan's well, St Govan's Head, Pembrokeshire.

The building consists of a simple nave with a stone altar, with benches and a piscina (or shallow basin with a drain, for washing the Communion vessels) built into the wall. There is a shelf, and a well in the floor, adjoining the north wall. Its water is said to cure eye diseases, skin complaints, and rheumatism. The chapel's arched roof, with its stone vault, is typical of early medieval churches in Pembrokeshire, and probably dates from the thirteenth century. The second well, in a stone well house on the shore below the chapel, is now dry. Govan is otherwise unknown; tradition describes him as an Irish monk who is said to have hidden here from pirates based on Lundy Island, which is 30 miles to the south and 10 miles off the Devon coast.

Hermits on Islands

Some hermits preferred to live on islands, where they could pray without disturbance. A number of small monastic sites are on islets connected to the mainland only at low tide. This enabled monks to combine solitude with easy access to centres of population. A monk named Cwyfan, who was said to be a disciple of St Beuno, gave his name to the tiny church on Llangwyfan, a tidal island off the Anglesey coast, north of Aberffraw. Cwyfan and Beuno will be described more fully in Chapter 7.

St Cwyfan's church, Llangwyfan, Anglesey.

Although Llangwyfan is now remote, this was once a relatively populous area, and the church was built on a peninsula between two streams. Over the centuries the surrounding land has been eroded, creating an island which is now a rocky outcrop in Caernarfon Bay. In 1802 John Skinner wrote:

> Llangwyfan church is erected on a rocky peninsula jutting out into the sea, and is an island at high water, so that not infrequently the congregation were interrupted in their devotion by the rapid approach of the waves.[21]

The island is less than an acre in area, and in summer the grass of the raised churchyard is studded with pink thrift and golden birdsfoot trefoil. The isolated rock is connected to the mainland at low tide by a causeway that is 200 m long. The single-chambered church dates from the fourteenth to the sixteenth century, and contains some Norman stonework. The Eucharist was celebrated here, when the tide and weather allowed, until a new church was built on the mainland in 1872.

The church is usually locked; to find it, take the A4080 out of Aberffraw, heading north-west for Holyhead. After a mile, turn left along a rough road into a motorbike-racing area. Go through its entrance kiosk, where you can check directions. Continue along the road, and fork right. Park where the road ends; Cwyfan's islet is ahead of you.

The *Black Book of Carmarthen*

Few early texts survive to tell us how monks and nuns lived, thought, and prayed in Celtic Wales. However, we can find some clues in the *Black Book of Carmarthen*, so-called because of its black binding. This is a sequence of poems which form the earliest collection of Welsh religious literature. It was probably compiled in the second half of the thirteenth century in a Cistercian monastery, or at the Augustinian Priory of St John the Evangelist in Carmarthen. However, the language of these monastic poems suggests that they were written earlier, perhaps in the late ninth or the tenth century. They offer insights into the hearts and minds of early Welsh Christians.

Some of the poems indicate how monks should live. One, entitled 'The Advice of Addaon', describes monks chanting the Our Father, the Creed, and the *Beati*. This is psalm 118 (119), the longest psalm, beginning *Beati immaculate in via* ('Blest are they whose way is blameless'). In an Old Irish list of Commutations, it could be recited many times, together with the Creed and the Our Father, as a substitute for the more severe penances prescribed in the Penitentials.

The poem continues to describe the importance of caring for the poor, by feeding the hungry and clothing the naked. 'The Advice of Addaon' begins:

> I asked all the priests of the world,
> the bishops and judges,
> what most profits the soul.
>
> The Lord's Prayer, the *Beati* and holy Creed,
> all sung for the sake of the soul,
> are best practised until Judgement Day.
>
> If only you shape your own path
> and build up peace,
> you shall see no end to mercy.
>
> Feed the hungry and clothe the naked,
> sing out in praise,
> for you have escaped the devil's number... [22]

The poem thus presents a programme of prayer and good works for the devout monk.

The *Céli Dé*, or *Clients of God*

By the eighth century, communities varied widely in their worship and practice, and there was a desire to return to the ascetic ideals of early monastic life. A leading figure in this movement was Máelrúain (d. 792), who founded a monastery at Tallaght (now a southern suburb of Dublin). The movement spread from Munster to other parts of Ireland, and as far as Iona; its monks became known as *Céli Dé*, meaning 'Clients (or Servants) of God'. They produced the earliest Irish religious lyrics, which form the closest literary parallels to a number of poems with a penitential theme in the *Black Book of Carmarthen*. These, too, convey a spirit of monastic reform. [23] Gerald of Wales tells us that there were *Céli Dé* monasteries in north-west Wales, at Beddgelert, Penmon, and on Bardsey Island.

The exhortatory tone of these poems suggests that they were perhaps written by Welsh *Céli Dé* living close to other monks whose life was less strict.[24] There is archaeological evidence of a *Céli Dé* community in south Wales at Burry Holms in the Gower peninsula, while monks at St David's and Llanbadarn Fawr had close links with Ireland. St David's might owe its austere, ascetical lifestyle to the influence of the *Céli Dé*, while Rhygyfarch's father, Sulien (who became bishop of St David's in 1073), was a native of Llanbadarn Fawr, and studied at length in Ireland.

It is possible that the *Black Book of Carmarthen* originated from either St David's or Llanbadarn Fawr, or indeed from both of these monasteries, which may well have transmitted Irish reforming monastic zeal to south-west Wales. The poems are written as advice to fellow monks; they are written in Welsh rather than Latin. Some of them may have been sung before or after the liturgy, or perhaps they were sung at community meals for entertainment and instruction.[25]

Poems of Praise

Besides the penitential poems in the *Black Book of Carmarthen*, there are a number of poems of praise. The word 'psalm' means 'praise', and monks rose early to praise God, and stayed awake at night to praise him. These poems are also influenced by secular Welsh praise poetry, which probably originated to celebrate the exploits of early medieval chieftains. This type of poetry flowered most fully in the twelfth and thirteenth centuries, when a bard acclaimed his ruler in return for lodging and maintenance, offering undying fame to his lord.[26]

Poets were highly respected in both Irish and Welsh society, and poetry had long been a medium of teaching and a form of public proclamation. In a passage from a poem in the *Black Book of Carmarthen* entitled 'Dispute between Body and Soul', the soul accuses the body of not having 'respected Friday' (by fasting), of not having 'sung the Our Father, matins and vespers', and of having failed to 'respect relics, monastery and the church'; however, the soul also adds that the body has not 'listened to the songs of clear-speaking poets'.[27] This is a unique statement in English, Irish or European literature: it indicates how highly secular poets were respected in early Christian Wales.[28] It also demonstrates that Welsh Christians deeply valued their native culture.

2

David, Non and Justinian

There was a strong Irish presence in south Wales in the fifth and sixth centuries. Later Irish legendary material claims that the Demetae, a tribe from southern Leinster, invaded south-west Wales and set up the kingdom of Demetia (or Dyfed in Welsh) in what is now Pembrokeshire and Carmarthenshire. It appears that Dyfed was ruled by an Irish dynasty between the fifth and eighth centuries.[1] Irish ogham stones and place names are found in Pembrokeshire, which indicates that some local people, possibly including David, spoke Irish as well as Welsh and Latin.

The earliest references to David are Irish: his feast is given in two Irish martyrologies (or calendars of saints), which date from about 800—the *Martyrology of Óengus the Culdee* lists the feast of 'David cille muni' (*cille muni* meaning 'church of Menevia') under 1 March, as does the *Martyrology of Tallaght*. A ninth- or tenth-century Catalogue of Irish Saints also names David as a source for an order of service 'from Dewi [David], Gildas and Docas'. The Irish Annals of Inisfallen and Tigernach report the 'repose of David of Cille Muine' in 589, but dates given in these sources are unreliable since the annals were compiled between the twelfth and the fifteenth centuries.[2]

From the eighth to the tenth centuries, David was considered as a guide to monastic living, and a 'Penitential of David' (or manual of punishments for crimes) is ascribed to him. Most of our knowledge about him comes from a *Life of David*, written by Rhygyfarch in about 1095. The author came from a distinguished family of scholarly monks and clerics who contributed to Welsh life and learning in Norman times.

Rhygyfarch's *Life of David*

Rhygyfarch's father had been bishop of St David's for ten years, and attended a meeting between William the Conqueror and two Welsh princes in 1081 at St David's. The Welsh chieftains probably appealed to William to uphold the independence of the Welsh Church against the increasing power of Rome. Rhygyfarch may have written his *Life of David* for this occasion, as a statement about the authority of their Church and the holiness of its founder.

Rhygyfarch tells us that David's father was Sant, ruler of the Welsh kingdom of Ceredigion, and his mother, from the neighbouring Irish kingdom of Dyfed to the south, across the River Teifi, was called Non. By presenting David's parents as coming from both kingdoms, Rhygyfarch conveyed that David was a national figure. It was seen as fitting that David's parents should be named Sant (from the Latin word *sanctus* or 'holy') and Non, meaning 'nun'. David is described as a great preacher, organiser, and inspirational leader, although these qualities clearly belong to Rhygyfarch's political agenda rather than to the historical David.

Like any other saint's Life, its primary purpose was to promote his cult; it presents a Rule of St David (chapters 21–31), written for use at St David's, and it also connects David with a ruling dynasty of Ceredigion by recording the genealogy of David (ch. 68). This links David to the line of Cunedda, the ancestor of the second dynasty of Gwynedd, from whom Rhys ap Tewdwr was descended.[3]

The *Life of David* is therefore likely to have been written when Rhys ap Tewdwr was still in power. In his later writings, Rhygyfarch does not favour the Normans, but his *Life of David* appears to predate such sentiments; this suggests that it was composed before 1093, when Rhys ap Tewdwr was defeated by 'the Frenchmen', the Normans living in Brecon, further to the east.[4]

Rhygyfarch's *Life of David* is permeated by quotations from the Old and New Testaments. Gildas is struck dumb in church at the presence of the unborn child, like Zecharaiah struck dumb in the temple at the conception of John the Baptist, in Luke's Gospel (ch. 5; see Luke 1. 8–23). An evil ruler vows to kill the child who will be the future saint, like King Herod in Matthew's Gospel, who massacres the Innocents (ch. 6; see Matthew 2. 1–19).[5] In this way, David is depicted as a holy man, with his life modelled on that of Jesus.

The Life also portrays David as Lord of Ceredigion: thirty years before David's birth, King Sant finds three gifts that indicate David's future property rights in the region (ch. 2): a stag, a fish, and a swarm of bees. These gifts confer on David the right to use the produce of forest, stream, and field. The three gifts are found 'next to the River Teifi … in a place called Llyn Henllan'; this is probably the village of Henllan on the Teifi, in Ceredigion.[6]

The Monastery at Henfynyw

According to his Life (chs. 8, 14), David was educated at and returned to *Vetus Rubus*, which was probably meant to indicate Henfynyw, just south of Aberaeron, on the coast road to Aberystwyth. Henfynyw means 'Old Menevia' in English, while the Welsh name for St David's was Fynyw, or '(new) Menevia'. The church at Henfynyw stands on a cliff overlooking the sea, beside a steep-sided valley where boats could land.

The monastery was known as a place of learning, under the leadership of a bishop named Guistilianus. An ancient well stood at the northern corner of the churchyard.[7] Henfynyw's location, 'near the banks of the Aeron with its clover-filled meadows and acorn-loaded trees', is described by the late twelfth-century poet Gwynfardd Brycheiniog in a lengthy poem in praise of David. The church is now rebuilt and the churchyard remodelled, but there are traces of a larger, irregular outer enclosure which indicate the monastic site.[8]

Above left: The cliff-top site of Henfynyw monastery, Aberaeron, Ceredigion.

Above right: Medieval font, Aberaeron church, Ceredigion.

A fragment of a large pillar stone was found at Henfynyw bearing the inscription 'TIGEIR...'—probably meaning '[the stone of] Tigernacus, or Tigernus'. It dates from about 550 to 750, during or soon after David's lifetime, and commemorates an Irish individual. The element *tigeirn* (or 'prince') is found in many names of the period, such as Vortigern, a British ruler, and the Scottish saint Kentigern. Tigernacus may have been an early abbot or holy man prominent in the community at Henfynyw.

Llanddewi Brefi

According to Rhygyfarch, David rose to a position of leadership during the Synod of Brefi (*c.* 545), which is presented as a religious gathering to refute the heretical teachings of Pelagius. This British theologian taught that people could reach heaven by their own efforts, without the help of God's grace. The gathering took place at what is now Llanddewi Brefi (or 'David's church beside the River Brefi'), which is on a mountain pass to the north of the Roman road from Carmarthen to the Roman fort of Bremia, at Llanio, a mile north-west of the church. The settlement was a natural place to assemble; three Roman roads converge nearby, and they continued in use long after the Romans departed, although by the mid-sixth century they were probably becoming overgrown.

At the synod, no one could make their voice heard over such a large crowd. David was a clear, convincing speaker, and he was brought from nearby to address the gathering.[9] From this time onwards, says Rhygyfarch, David began to be seen as a bishop. He wore rough clothes and carried a large branch rather than a crosier. Rhygyfarch relates that he went about bareheaded and barefoot, carrying a bell which he named *bangu* (or 'dear, loud one').

Rhygyfarch describes the synod as an imposing event attended by 118 bishops from across Britain:

> Then, at an appointed place called Brefi ... they each endeavoured to preach ... Then [David] made his way to the synod. The assembly of bishops rejoiced, the people were glad, and the whole gathering exulted ... the earth under him swelled and was raised to a hill ... A church is situated on the top of that hill now.[10]

The purpose of Rhygyfarch's story of the synod is to present David as a national figure. The synod may well have taken place, since this would be a suitable location, but with a smaller number of bishops attending.

The church 'on the top of that hill' is probably built on a prehistoric mound, and is a typical monastic site—a virtual island, with a stream flowing along one side. In time, the monastery is likely to have extended to the flat area below the hilltop, where there would have been more space for a scriptorium and other buildings. By the ninth century, Llanddewi Brefi had become a *clas* community of non-celibate clerics living a monastic type of life; it remained a *clas* church until the early 1200s. *Clasau* were wealthy churches, some of whose members would be more involved in the local community, while others remained more isolated.

Monuments to Early Monks

There are a number of early Christian monuments at Llanddewi Brefi that would have been pillars in the churchyard—conspicuous monuments to founding figures, abbots, and holy men of the monastery. Perhaps the earliest is a fragmentary pillar stone. The antiquarian Edward Lhuyd (1660–1709) concluded that it read: 'HIC IACET IDNERT FILIVS I[ACOBI] QUI OCCISVS FVIT PROPTER [PREDAM] SANCTI [DAVID]', or 'Here lies Jacob, son of Idnert, who was slain on account of the flock [or herd] of holy David'.

'Flock' could be read literally or figuratively, and although the inscription was once dated to the mid-seventh century, linguistic reasons might make a ninth-century date more likely.[11] Idnert was probably a member of the community who died when the monastery was sacked. Two fragments of this large inscribed stone can be seen in the exterior west wall of the church, on the north side.

A seventh-century memorial stone to Dallus Dumelus was described in chapter one. Since his two names are Irish, this suggests that Irish monks left their nearby clan-

kingdom of Dyfed to the south, and went into exile by joining this monastery across the River Teifi in Ceredigion, where Irish names appear only in a religious context. A simpler pillar, which dates from the seventh to the ninth century, bears a Latin cross with curving feet and arm-ends, giving it, perhaps unintentionally, the appearance of a little person.

A later pillar stone, almost 6 feet tall, commemorates a ninth-century abbot or senior figure in the monastery from around the time that it became a *clas* community. At the top of the pillar is a long Latin cross which, like those on the other monuments, has little bars on the cross ends—this was a local style. Beneath the cross, an inscription reads downwards: 'CENLISINI B[ENEDICAT] D[EUS]', or '[the stone of] Cenlisinus, God bless him'. The Latin contractions, or abbreviations, of the words *benedicat* and *Deus* and the fully uncial book hand indicate that the mason was a literate monk used to writing manuscripts, and that the memorial is carved for a monastic audience used to reading written texts.

It is possible that the twelfth-century poet Gwynfardd Brycheiniog's poem in praise of David, entitled *Canu Dewi*, was composed for an audience assembled at Llanddewi Brefi for a feast day, perhaps when the Lord Rhys was present. Gwynfardd describes 'The five altars of Brefi in honour of the saints' (l. 269), which suggests the various churches often found at an early medieval monastic site. He also praises Brefi's *braint* (privilege) describing its entitlements, and its *nawdd* (sanctuary), for it was a place where criminals could take refuge from the law.[12]

Above left: Latin cross, Llanddewi Brefi, Ceredigion.

Above right: Memorial to Cenlisinus, Llanddewi Brefi, Ceredigion.

David's Monastic Rule

Chapters 21 to 31 of Rhygyfarch's *Life of David* describe how he established a monastery at St David's where, together with his disciples, he followed an austere life 'in imitation of the monks of Egypt' (ch. 31). David chose a site in the narrow valley of the River Alun, hidden from pirates by a bend in the river. A section of Rhygyfarch's Life draws on an early source and relates how the monks grew their food, working hard with mattocks, hoes, and axes. They ploughed the fields themselves, instead of using oxen (ch. 22), and spent the rest of the day reading, writing, and praying.

In the evening they gathered in the church for vespers, and then prayed silently until night fell. Only then would they eat together: a simple meal of 'bread and herbs, seasoned with salt' (ch. 24), eaten in moderation and washed down with ale. David himself lived on bread, vegetables, and water. After their frugal meal, the monks returned to chapel to pray for another few hours (ch. 25). Following a short night's sleep, they woke at cock-crow to sing matins and to 'spend the rest of the night until morning without sleep' (ch. 26).

Anyone seeking to join the community was to be kept waiting outside the door for ten days, to test his desire for monastic life. The candidate was then welcomed by the doorkeeper, and put to work alongside the monks for many months, 'until the natural stubbornness of his heart was broken' (ch. 29). The pattern of life in David's monastery was unusually severe.

When Rhygyfarch relates how David's disciples 'would place the yoke upon their shoulders; they would push spades and shovels into the earth with their unfailing arms' (ch. 22), this possibly originates from David's actual Rule. The sixth-century theologian Gildas appears to quote this portion of the Rule in a surviving fragment of a letter to Finnian, when he described monks who 'drag ploughs and dig in the ground with mattocks in presumption and pride'. The Irish monk Columbanus cites this letter when writing to Pope Gregory the Great in AD 600.[13]

As a Benedictine monk, however, Pope Gregory the Great is likely to have preferred the more moderate Rule of Benedict. It is significant that the asceticism of David's Rule was sufficiently well-known to feature in international correspondence between major Church figures. The rigour of David's Rule appears to grow out of an ascetic tradition in south Wales, which is found also in the seventh-century *Life of Samson*.[14]

Bishop Asser

The first English references to David are found in the writings of Asser (d. 909), who wrote a biography of King Alfred the Great. Asser was invited from the 'most western parts of Wales' in 885 to become Bishop of Sherborne in Dorset; he tells us that a relative of his named Nobis has been archbishop of the monastery and territory of St David. It is apparent that David was already a prominent saint and the monastery at St David's had a wide reputation for learning.[15] In Asser's own words, he came to England so that King Alfred's literary programme might 'benefit in every respect from the learning of St David'.[16]

In the eighth and ninth centuries the cult of David, based at Menevia, was both powerful and extensive. Asser's kinsman, Archbishop Nobis, would have been overlord of the kingdom of Dyfed—an important role, similar to that of the bishop of Armagh in northern Ireland. From the fifth to the tenth centuries, Dyfed seems to have been divided into smaller units, *cantrefi*, which were perhaps smaller kingdoms ruled by kings, based on Irish models. By now, in the late ninth or early tenth century, these small kingdoms appear to have evolved into seven 'bishop-houses' that are referred to in later Welsh laws: Menevia, and six others named after local holy men.[17]

St David's Cathedral

The low-lying, marshy site of St David's cathedral is typical of an early monastery; its nucleus was probably around the transept of the present cathedral. Lower down the hill, the river would have flooded the site. Excavation has provided no evidence of a pre-Norman church or churches, although part of a wheel-headed cross and fine, decorated, carved stone fragments indicate the quality of the eleventh- and twelfth-century church. All the archaeological finds have been of high medieval date, contemporary with the present cathedral. The north chapel is at a slight angle to the rest of the cathedral, which suggests that it was aligned with earlier structures.

The monastery was destroyed many times; anonymous raiders attacked St David's in 810 and 907, while Vikings raided the site in 988, a year in which they also attacked Llanbadarn Fawr, Llancarfan, and Llanilltud Fawr. Vikings again attacked St David's in 999, when they killed its bishop, Morgeneu. Gerald of Wales (*c.* 1146–1223), who wished to become bishop of St David's but failed to be appointed, recounts a vision received by an Irish bishop in which Morgeneu pointed to his wounds and said, 'Because I ate flesh, flesh [i.e. carrion] I am become.' This implies that the community had remained faithful to the ascetic tradition of not eating meat, until Morgeneu relaxed this rule.[18]

The Saxons raided St David's in 1011; in 1022 and 1073 there were raids by two different pirates named Eilaf. In a raid of 1080, Bishop Abraham was killed, and Sulien of Llanbadarn Fawr was recalled as bishop for a second time. In 1091 'the men of the Isles' destroyed Menevia, and Gerald of Wales' own grandfather, Gerald of Windsor, ravaged the boundaries of Menevia in 1097. The *Life of Caradoc* recounts that because of attacks by pirates from the Orkneys, St David's was almost uninhabited for seven years, and a visitor took almost a week to get to David's tomb 'because of the thorns and briars' that now covered the deserted site.[19]

Despite the cathedral's repeated destruction, by the tenth century David was presented as a national figure; verses in the prophetic poem *Armes Prydein* declare him to be the chief intercessor of the saints of Wales. The Normans took over both the site and the cult of St David, and since David was seen as a focus for resistance against the Normans, they invested heavily in the site. David's cult was promoted in the eleventh and twelfth centuries as Menevia struggled to achieve supremacy among Welsh bishoprics.

St David's cathedral, Pembrokeshire.

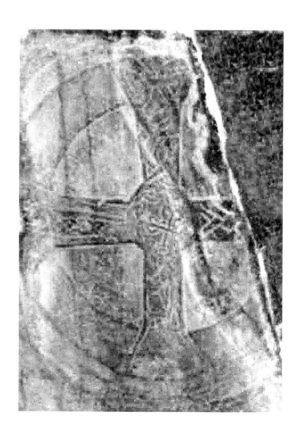

An early cross, St David's,
Pembrokeshire.

St David's was surrounded by a number of subsidiary chapels—most of them near the shore, where pilgrims would land. Architectural details of ruins at these sites suggest a late medieval date, but most of them originated as earlier Christian cemeteries. They were developed by and for David's cult, long after his death, through locating supposed incidents from his life at chapels, holy wells, and other features in the landscape. In the high Middle Ages, the town's name was changed from Menevia (from the Irish for a thorny bush or thicket) to Ty-Dewi ('David's house').[20] Today, twenty-seven parish churches, thirty-seven chapels, and thirty-one wells are dedicated to David.[21]

David's Relics

There are no early accounts of St David's relics; Rhygyfarch simply relates that David died and was buried at his monastery. The twelfth-century *Brut y Twysogyon* (or *Chronicle of the Princes*) relates that a reliquary and other valuables were stolen from the church in 1089, during a period of disorder, on account of their gold and silver, 'and [were] completely despoiled near the city'.[22] Order was restored, however, and the *Chronicle of the Princes* also records that in 1171, en route to Ireland, King Henry II went on pilgrimage to St David's, where he 'made an offering of two choral copes of brocaded silk for the use of cantors to serve God and David'.[23]

St David's relics were venerated at the cathedral in the eleventh century, since in 1081 Gruffudd ap Cynan (King of Gwynedd) and Rhys ap Tewdwr 'went together to the church of David to pray. There they became faithful friends, after swearing on the relics'.[24] Other personal possessions associated with David were his bell, once kept at Glascwm, Montgomeryshire, and his staff, formerly preserved at Llanddewi Brefi.[25]

In response to a new demand for physical relics, David's body was 'discovered' as the result of a dream by the Prior of Ewenny in Glamorgan, and a new shrine was constructed in 1275. The reliquary contained within the shrine is likely to have been a small casket, despite the large shrine's resemblance to those containing a saint's body. The dish-like receptacles behind its quatrefoil openings were probably intended for gifts of money—a unique feature in a shrine of this type.

King Edward I and Queen Eleanor visited the shrine in 1284, when the king was given an arm bone of David. The *Black Book of St Davids*, compiled in 1324, records that in time of war, both English and Welsh tenants of St David's 'are bound to follow the Lord Bishop with the shrine of the Blessed David with the relics'.[26]

At the Reformation, William Barlow, the recently-appointed Bishop of St David's, seized the relics when they were brought out for display on St David's Day, 1 March 1538. In a letter to Thomas Cromwell, he describes the 'fayned relics' as follows: 'two heedes [heads] of sylver plate enclosing two rotten skulles studded with putrified clowtes [cloths]; Item, two arme bones, and a worme eaten boke covered with sylver plate'.[27] Perhaps the 'worme eaten boke' was an illuminated manuscript like the Lichfield Gospels or the Book of Kells.

St Non's Chapel, St David's

Rhygyfarch does not give a location for David's birth—he merely recounts that a rock bearing the imprint of Non's hands, made during her birth pangs, was incorporated into the altar of a church built on the spot (ch. 6). It seems to have been Gerald of Wales, writing in the twelfth century, who located David's birthplace at St Non's chapel on the coast, a mile south of St David's. The late medieval chapel is located within an earlier earth-banked enclosure. In the foreground of colour plate 1 is one of a group of Bronze Age boulders outside St Non's chapel.

The lower strata of the chapel walls are of cyclopean masonry: these huge stone blocks are often found in seventh- to eighth-century Anglo-Saxon buildings. There may have been a pre-Christian cemetery here, which later became a Christian one. Nineteenth-century excavations revealed cist (or slab-lined) graves, to the east and south of the chapel, near the standing stones. Some of the graves date from between the seventh and ninth century, suggesting that this was a burial chapel in an extramural cemetery outside St David's. Inside the chapel, a gravestone carved with a simple ringed cross dates from the same period.

Sadly, much of the chapel was demolished in 1810; nearby farmers used the stone to repair their field boundaries.[28] St Non's chapel is one of the eight medieval oratories dotted around the headlands of St David's peninsula, each within a few miles of the cathedral. Pilgrims travelled here by sea from north Wales, southern Ireland, Cornwall, and Brittany. They climbed up from the shore below to give thanks for their safe arrival, for their small boats were at the mercy of winds, tides, and the many currents around the coast.

St Non's chapel, St Non's Bay, Pembrokeshire.

Latin ringed cross, St Non's chapel, St Non's Bay,
Pembrokeshire.

Navigators could not always choose where to land, but there are small harbours near each
chapel with paths leading to St David's.[29]

Non's Holy Well

Close to St Non's chapel is her holy well. This is one of the chief healing wells of Wales; it
was famous for curing eye diseases. Holy wells were often visited for eye ailments because
pure spring water was essential to cleanse infected eyes. In the early eighteenth century,
Browne Willis wrote:

> There is a fine well … covered with a stone roof and enclosed within a wall, with benches
> to sit upon round the well. Some old, simple people go still to visit this saint. … especially
> upon St Nun's day [3 March], which they keep holy and [they] offer pins, pebbles etc at
> this well.[30]

A century later, the well was still popular, as Richard Fenton reported:

> The fame this consecrated spring had obtained is incredible, and still it is resorted to
> for many complaints. In my infancy … I was often dipped in it, and offerings, however
> trifling, even a farthing or a pin, were made after each ablution, and the bottom of the
> well shone with votive brass.[31]

St Non's well, St Non's Bay, Pembrokeshire.

In the field leading to the chapel, there was a cottage for the well's caretaker. The well-house was restored in 1951.

The Role of St Non

There are a significant number of saints who are mothers and who come from noble families in the Lives of Welsh saints. The importance of family relationships is stressed in early genealogies, often creating a network of related saints. David's grandmother, Meleri, was said to be one of the twenty-four daughters of Brychan, all of whom were Welsh mothers of male saints.[32] Non figures in hagiography purely as the mother of St David. Most of what is told about her derives from the various versions of Rhygyfarch's *Life of David*, while other sources include Middle Welsh poetry and local folklore. It may be that, along with mothers in other saints' Lives, the figure of Non was invented in order to elaborate the story of David's birth.[33]

Unlike most Welsh female saints, Non is commemorated at several locations in south Wales, and also in Brittany, Ireland, Cornwall, and Devon; in Wales, her feast is listed in most medieval Welsh calendars. Non is a rare example of a raped female saint; in the saints' Lives, many virgins fled arranged marriages or were abducted, tortured, or killed, but few were actually raped. However, particularly in medieval hagiography in the Celtic regions, the violation of a nun was sometimes deemed appropriate in order to explain the conception of a powerful male saint, while a raped virgin could be considered more heroic, in that she conceived without experiencing sexual pleasure.[34]

If Non existed, it is not inconceivable that she might have been a nun, as were most early Christian female saints in the Celtic lands. St Non was seen as holy because of her relationship with her holy son, in a role similar to that of Mary within the Holy Family. Perhaps because of her role as a maternal saint, Non offered a closer model for medieval married women than the virgin saints. In the poetry of the *Cywyddwyr* (or 'poets of the nobility'), composed from about 1330 onwards, married noblewomen are more frequently compared to Non than to any other female saint, apart from Our Lady.[35]

Non's Cult in Brittany

There is no Welsh Life of St Non, but a late medieval Breton miracle play, *Buez Santez Nonn hac ez map Deuy* ('The Life of St Non and of her son David'), survives in a fifteenth-century manuscript, probably written by a monk of the abbey of Daoulas.[36] It expands upon the brief account of Non in the Latin and Welsh Lives of David, giving a lengthy and dramatic account of Non's rape, and relocates most of the story to Brittany. It claims that Non was born of 'powerful people from Brittany, nobles of a rich house', and that she lived and died at Dirinon, where her bones were interred.[37] Dirinon is 3 miles north of Daoulas.

The *Buez* relates that Non was buried in a new tomb at Dirinon. The Life was evidently composed shortly after it was built, in order to emphasise Dirinon's new status and the importance of its tomb and its patrons. It is likely that the monument, in a sixteenth-century chapel beside the parish church, was commissioned by Simon de Kerbringal and Maufuric de Lézuzan, Abbot of Daoulas, who died in 1468. However, when the tomb was later taken apart and reconstructed, it was found to contain only a few bones of an adolescent.[38] Non is carved recumbent on her fine granite tomb; she clasps a book in her hand, while two angels hold the corners of her pillow.

Non's tomb and the *Buez* appear to have been commissioned when a significant relic of Non was acquired. Her reliquary can be found in Dirinon parish church; two fragments of shin bone, wrapped in silk, are contained in a silver gilt shrine that is thought to have been made in Morlaix in around 1450. The reliquary is designed in the shape of a chapel, with stone walls, traceried windows, and a tiled roof, surmounted by a small silver statue of David with mitre and crosier (see photo opposite).

Llannon and Aberarth

Returning to south Wales, the church at Llannon, 4 miles north-east of Aberaeron on the Ceredigion coast, may also be dedicated to Non; however, the settlement's name may derive from *llan* and *on(n)*, meaning 'church of the ash tree'.[39] Three miles south-west of Llannon, there was a monastery named after David on the coast at Llanddewi Aberarth, where the River Arth meets the sea. There is no harbour, but one could land on the beach; Viking ships may have drawn up here, and Norsemen may have settled the area. Part

St Non's reliquary (1450), Dirinon, Brest, Brittany.

Fragment of Viking hogback tomb, Llanddewi Aberarth, Ceredigion.

of a mid- or late tenth-century Viking hogback tomb is preserved in the church on the headland high above, and may indicate the burial of a local lord.

The position and irregular shape of the churchyard suggest that it originally might have been an Iron Age promontory fort. On the beach below there are extensive early-medieval fish traps in the area between high and low tide, perhaps devised by the monastic community. All that survives from the monastery are two fragments of a ninth- or tenth-century inscribed and decorated cross shaft.[40] In the nineteenth century, however, four other early Christian monuments were said to have been found here.[41] By the thirteenth century, this was a chapel belonging to the church at Aberaeron.

The Cult of David and Non in Cornwall

There are nine ancient churches named after David in Cornwall, including that of Davidstow, on the edge of Bodmin Moor. This bleak moorland village is 12 miles west of Launceston. Its former name was Dewstow—David's name is *Dewi Sant* in Welsh. There are some fine thirteenth-century carved bench ends in the church, including a rare depiction of a minstrel blowing the Cornish bagpipes; these instruments were played in Celtic times. St David's holy well is in a field to the east of the church, clearly signed from the road. The rectangular pool is protected by a modern stone well-house. Its water is so pure that it is used by the local creamery, whose mild Davidstow cheese is widely sold.

Seven miles south-east of Davidstow, the settlement of Altarnun ('Non's altar') is dedicated to David's mother. She is honoured with a fine church here, lying beside a fast-flowing stream in a valley. There is a tall Celtic cross in the churchyard, and it may have been a pre-Christian monolith. In a field above the church, Non's holy well feeds a bowssening pool. This is a pond into which the insane were tumbled in a primitive form of shock therapy. They were then taken down to the church, where Masses were sung for their recovery.[42]

Non may also be remembered in south-east Cornwall at Pelynt, 4 miles west of Looe. Its name comes from *plou Nent*, which means 'parish of Non'. Pelynt is the only example of a Cornish church name that incorporates the word *plou*, although it is often found in Brittany.[43] *Plou* is an early word derived from the Latin *plebs*, meaning 'the people [of God]'. Non's holy well is a mile east of Pelynt, above the River Duloe, where a spring emerges from the hillside in Hobb Park. Although restored, the well-house retains its original shape, with a curved roof, a stone lintel, and walls of flat, unmortared stones. On either side of the entrance is a stone bench where pilgrims could sit and pray.

Inside the well-house, water trickles into a heavy bowl of pink granite, incised with wheel crosses; it dates from early times. A hundred years ago, the outline of a mound and wall could still be traced above the well: this may have been a chapel.[44] There is a third holy well dedicated to Non at St Mawgan-in-Pydar, near the north Cornish coast, 5 miles north-east of Newquay.

St Justinian

Justinian is an early saint who lived near St David's. Lives of the saints often explained the proximity of dedications by making a less famous saint a disciple of, or confessor to, a more famous saint whose cult-site lay nearby. An example of this can be seen in the legends, chapel, shrine, and dedications associated with Justinian (or 'Stinan' in Welsh). On the east side of Ramsey Island, facing the mainland south of St David's, was a chapel dedicated to St Justinian, across the narrow but treacherous Ramsey Sound, close to a spring at a landing place.[45]

The fourteenth-century 'Life of Justinian' is found in a collection entitled *Nova Legenda Angliae*, compiled by John of Tynemouth, who probably derived his account from an earlier source at St David's. We are told that Justinian came from Brittany and joined other hermits on Ramsey Island. His ascetic lifestyle attracted disciples, and so great was his reputation that he became David's confessor. He was killed by his servants, who disliked his strict regime; a spring, which healed the sick, emerged from the spot where he was beheaded. John of Tynemouth relates that its water 'quaffed by sick folk, conveys health of body to all'.[46]

Although dead, Justinian walked across the Sound to Porth Stinan, where he was buried, and a chapel was built over his tomb; St David then translated his friend's body to his own church. It is not know when Justinian's relics were brought to St David's. Medieval pilgrims crossed to Ramsey Island, particularly to visit its miraculous well. Many of the incidents in the 'Life of Justinian' are themes commonly found in other saints' Lives, interwoven with local topographical details, and although the relationship between David and Justinian might sound convincing, Rhygyfarch does not mention Justinian in his *Life of David*, nor is he mentioned in the twelfth- and thirteenth-century versions of David's Life.

Justinian's Chapel at Porth Stinan

This chapel on the mainland facing Ramsey Island, 2 miles west of St David's, was restored by Bishop Vaughan in the early sixteenth century (see overleaf). Excavations in 1926 revealed a late twelfth-century chancel and nave, with a special grave in the southern half of the chancel, to the right of the altar; there were a number of other burials in the chancel. The elaborate slab-lined grave was covered with white quartz pebbles; this overlay an earlier grave, which was cut by the north wall of the building.[47] It was customary to bring white pebbles to a saint's tomb; the elaborate grave could be that of Justinian. His holy well, known for its healing properties, is beside the road near the chapel.

Ramsey Island

Porth Stinan was the embarkation point for pilgrims to visit Ramsey Island. There was an early Christian cemetery on the island: in the late eighteenth century, the antiquarian

St Justinian's chapel, opposite Ramsey Island, Pembrokeshire.

Richard Fenton was shown 'a burying ground' uncovered by workmen digging foundations for the present farmhouse. The 'coffins' which he described were long-cists—slab-lined graves with a base formed of slabs and stone lintels covering them. Further graves were found in 1860, and more graves and 'headstones' were uncovered during building work in 1963.[48]

In 1967 an inscribed stone was spotted among the debris: a thin slate slab, inscribed 'S[.]TVRNBIV', above which are drilled terminals to the lines of what must have been a sundial. Saturnbiu Hael ('the Generous') is the first documented bishop of St David's; his death was recorded in 831 in the *Annales Cambriae*.[49] The presence of a sundial suggests a monastic community, who would need a device to tell the time in order to punctuate their day with prayer. Ramsey is likely to have served as an island retreat for the community at St David's.

St Justinian's Church, Llanstinan

This is an early church dedicated to Justinian in the valley of the River Cleddau, 10 miles north-east of St David's. It is built inside an ancient stone circle; seven springs are said to rise on the site, which was once beside a lake. The village of Scleddau, which surrounded the church, has now disappeared, although rambler roses from cottage gardens still grow in the hedgerows. The medieval church is built on early foundations, and has a 'squinch' (or small, triangular room) between the nave and the chancel, on the site where a hermit's cell adjoined the church.

Small, triangular room (left) for a hermit, Llanstinan, Pembrokeshire.

By living in a small room built against the church wall, a medieval hermit could retain his privacy and yet also be present at church services. A squinch is a feature of a number of early Pembrokeshire churches. Llanstinan is 2 miles south-east of Fishguard, near the A40. To find the church, after leaving Fishguard, watch for a sign to Llanstinan on the left, beside a disused quarry. Park in the lay-by, then walk for ten minutes along a signed footpath, through the Cleddau valley. Turn left through a farmyard; the church is on low ground in front of you.

3

Three Monks of South-West Wales: Padarn, Brynach and Teilo

Three early saints whose cult developed in south-west Wales were Padarn, Brynach and Teilo. Despite the increasing authority of St David's in the medieval period, the monasteries of these three monks at Llanbadarn Fawr, Nevern and Llandeilo Fawr attained considerable importance. We know little about their founding abbots apart from what is found in their late medieval Lives, but each monastery made a significant contribution to religious life in Wales—particularly Llanbadarn Fawr, with its tradition of scholarship.

Llanbadarn Fawr

It is possible that Padarn was an early bishop, and that Llanbadarn Fawr was a lesser bishopric. Padarn's name derives from the Latin *Paternus*, meaning 'Fatherly'; this was a common Latin name. There are seven known dedications to him. According to his twelfth-century Life, Padarn persuaded the local chieftain to give him land between the rivers Rheidol and Clarach, where he built the monastery of Llanbadarn Fawr on a hillside, in what is now a southern suburb of Aberystwyth. The site is near *Sarn Helen*, an ancient route continuing the line of the Roman coastal road; the trackway is named after Elen Luyddoc, who was said to be the wife of Magnus Maximus.

A tall, 3-m-high, narrow pillar cross survives from the monastery at Llanbadarn Fawr; it is carved from granite, perhaps brought from the Llŷn peninsula, and may date from the tenth century. The entire cross is richly decorated with abstract patterns, apart from a panel depicting a bishop with a mitre and a round-headed crosier, perhaps intended to represent Padarn. This is one of the few Welsh crosses on which figurative carving is found. A smaller, broader cross may date from the same period; both may be re-used pre-Christian standing stones.

The Meaning of *llan*

The English translation of Llanbadarn Fawr is 'Padarn's great church'. The meaning of the prefix *llan* evolved over time—the Celtic root word for *llan* originally meant 'land', but the

Tenth-century pillar cross, Llanbadarn Fawr, Ceredigion.

Carved cross, Llanbadarn Fawr, Ceredigion.

word came to mean 'enclosed land', as in *perllan* ('orchard') and *corlan* ('sheepfold'). *Llan* then successively came to mean: 'an enclosed cemetery'; 'the church within an enclosed cemetery'; and 'the area of land served by the church', or 'the parish'. Over centuries, it then came to mean 'the township surrounding a parish church', 'the farm next to the church', or simply 'church'.[1]

The prefix *llan* has been employed as a name-element from early medieval times onwards, and so it does not always indicate an early site, but it was chiefly used between the ninth and the eleventh centuries, when it described a monastic enclosure and, by extension, the monastery itself. The name-element is limited to Wales, Cornwall, and Brittany, with a few outliers, including Landican (Cheshire), *Lantokai* (now Street, in Somerset) and *Lanprobus* (now Sherborne, Dorset). It is possible that a number of *llan* place-names record the name of the patron or founder of the church, rather than that of an otherwise unrecorded local saint.[2]

A Powerful Community

Llanbadarn Fawr had close links with Ireland, and it may have become a reformed community—reflecting the influence of the Irish *Céli Dé* (or '*Clients of God*')—as did St David's. Llanbadarn Fawr became a centre of learning: by the eleventh century, under Abbot Sulien the Wise, its library was larger than those of Canterbury Cathedral or York Minster. Sulien was twice bishop of St David's; his four sons also became monks at Llanbadarn Fawr. The eldest, Rhygyfarch, wrote the *Life of David* that we examined in Chapter 2.

During the tenth and eleventh centuries, Welsh monasteries consolidated their power through receiving grants of land and income from pilgrimages. A late eleventh-century poem recounts that St Padarn's crosier known as *Cyrwen* (or 'holy staff with crooked head') was preserved at Llanbadarn Fawr, to be venerated by pilgrims. Larger and more-powerful communities assumed control of smaller ones that were founded by them or donated to them by local nobility: Llanbadarn Fawr had over twenty daughter houses.[3]

The parish of Llanbadarn Fawr was once the largest in Wales. Part of a cartulary was attached to the medieval *Life of Padarn*, in the form of charters and records of grants of land made to the monastery. The church had a *noddfa* or place of refuge for those fleeing from the law.[4] Abbots were both secular and spiritual leaders; Gerald of Wales describes the lay abbot of Llanbadarn Fawr and his retinue arriving to celebrate a feast day, armed with long spears.[5] The monastery was a *clas* community, a type of pre-Conquest Welsh monastery, and remained so until the twelfth or thirteenth century.

The word *clas* derives from the Latin *classis*, meaning a group or gathering of people. In Wales it described a group of clerics who lived in community, before monasteries were reorganised to follow a more structured Rule—such as those of St Benedict or St Augustine, which were introduced from the eleventh century onwards. The leaders of *clas* communities are described as abbots; the abbot's property was meant to be inherited by the *clas*.[6]

The Family of Sulien

Sulien the Wise (1011–91), of the house of Llanbadarn Fawr, was renowned as a teacher and advisor to bishops and kings; his name means 'born on a Sunday'. Sulien was twice bishop of St David's—once from 1072/3 to 1078 and again from 1080 to 1085. He had four sons: Rhygyfarch (meaning 'Praise of the King'), Arthgen (or 'Bear Cub'), Deiniol, and Ieuan. The last two were named after Daniel, the Old Testament prophet, and John, the fourth evangelist.[7] Sulien apparently took part in negotiations between Rhys ap Tewdwr and Gruffudd ap Cynan in 1081, and would have met William the Conqueror that same year. Towards the end of Rhygyfarch's *Life of David*, a lament over the dead saint appears to be a lament for Rhygyfarch's own father, Sulien, as well [8]:

> O who could then endure the weeping of the holy men, the deep sighing of the hermits, the wailing of the priests, and the moaning of the disciples, saying, 'By whom shall we be taught?'; the lamentation of pilgrims, saying, 'By whom shall we be assisted?'; the desperation of kings,

saying, 'By whom shall we be ordained, corrected, appointed?' … The voice of the mourners was but one, for kings honoured him as a judge, the older people mourned him as a brother, the younger honoured him as a father, indeed all venerated him as they did God.[9]

A group of late eleventh- and early twelfth-century manuscripts survive that were probably created by Sulien's sons at Llanbadarn Fawr. They include a copy of St Augustine's *De Trinitate* (*On the Trinity*) made by Sulien's son Ieuan, containing a Latin poem to his father entitled 'Ieuan's poem on the life and family of Sulien'. A psalter with a martyrology was illustrated by Ieuan, probably in around 1079; it was owned by Ieuan's brother, Rhygyfarch. Another manuscript contains a version of Macrobius's *Commentary* on Cicero's *Dream of Scipio*, together with two poems by Rhygyfarch. Fragments of a copy of Bede's *De Natura Rerum* also survive.[10] These illustrate the broad range of study undertaken at the monastery.

The psalter owned by Rhygyfarch and Augustine's *De Trinitate* contain the finest illuminations, which are mainly elaborate initials; the psalter also has three decorated pages which show similarities to the Lichfield Gospels created two centuries earlier in Ireland or Mercia. These books are some of the last products of a British school of manuscript production; their Insular minuscule script was soon to be replaced by Carolingian minuscule, brought by monks from mainland Europe, as Norman influence increased.[11]

Compositions by Sulien's Family

Besides copies of earlier texts, works written by Sulien and his oldest and youngest sons survive. Sulien composed a Life of the Irish saint Maedoc of Ferns, or at least introduced it into Wales. As we have seen, Rhygyfarch wrote a Life of David in Latin, as well as three Latin poems entitled 'On the Psalter', 'On an unhappy harvest' and 'Rhygyfarch's Lament', conveying his sadness about the Norman conquest of Wales. Sulien's youngest son, Ieuan, wrote a Latin Life of St Padarn and three Latin poems—'Ieuan's Invocation', 'Song about the Life and Family of Sulien', and 'Ieuan's Distichs'. He also wrote an *englyn*, a type of verse in Old Welsh, about St Padarn's staff, venerated in the church.[12]

The works written by Sulien and his sons appear to use simple language, but their construction is extremely complex. This is particularly true of Rhygyfarch's *Life of David*: its prologue of six lines is composed in Cicero's literary style, in its metre and its rhythm of stressed and unstressed syllables. Throughout the book, line endings rhyme in complex patterns. David Howlett has highlighted Rhygyfarch's formidable use of numerical symbolism—the six syllables of the title of the book are followed by six lines of the prologue, leading to six sentences in Chapter One, symbolising the days of the working week. The fifty-two letters of the subtitle precede the fifty-two words of the prologue, which may represent the fifty-two weeks of the year. The prologue's 365 letters relate to the 365 days of the year.[13]

In ancient Hebrew, Greek, and Latin texts, numerical values could also be assigned to words and to proper names. Rhygyfarch's brother Ieuan states in an acrostic poem that he uses this system, a literary device known as gematria. In his *Life of David*, Rhygyfarch employs gematria to an extraordinary extent, although the narrative appears straightforward and flowing. The same love of arithmetic complexity in prose can be found in many other Welsh-Latin texts from the fifth to the fifteenth century, on inscriptions, in diplomatic documents, and in literary works.[14] Rhygyfarch's immensely skilful style indicates the high level of accomplishment to be found in the monastery at Llanbadarn Fawr.

Tenderness in Monastic Life

At the same time, Rhygyfarch's *Life of David* displays tenderness; it is a labour of love. Rhygyfarch's monastic experience is likely to have been stable and affirming as he lived and prayed alongside his father and his three brothers, among many others. In a number of saints' Lives, an extended family, including uncles, aunts, and cousins, travels together in search of a new place to work and pray. Every week, monks and nuns chant psalm 132, which begins:

> How good and how pleasant it is,
> brothers dwelling in unity.

There is a tender, compassionate bond within a group who learn about God from each other, with a blend of intimacy and respect between a disciple and his or her teacher. Rhygyfarch conveys this when he describes young David's relationship with his supposed teacher, Paulinus:

> While the holy David was with his teacher Paulinus, it came about that the latter lost the sight of his eyes because of their great pain. He called each of his disciples in turn to inspect and bless his eyes; they did as he had told them, but he did not receive a cure from any of them. At last he summoned the holy David to him and said to him, 'Holy David, look closely at my eyes, because they are tormenting me'. And the holy David responded and said, 'My father, do not ask me to look at your face, because for ten years I have given my attention with you to scripture, and so far I have not looked at your face'. And Paulinus, admiring his extreme modesty, said. 'Since it is so, it will be sufficient for you to touch my eyes and bless them, and I shall be cured'. And as soon as he touched them—in a twinkling—his eyes were cured.[15]

Rhygyfarch here conveys the power of David's love, which heals the teacher who has given him so much; there is a mutual bond of tender respect. Rhygyfarch also recalls the loving actions of their master, Jesus, who twice healed a blind man by touching his eyes (Mt. 9. 29; 20. 34). This episode in Rhygyfarch's *Life of David* will be returned to in Chapter 5, when we consider the identity of Paulinus.

St Brynach's Church, Nevern

The chief church of St Brynach is at Nevern, 8 miles east of Fishguard, near the north Pembrokeshire coast. His title, *Brynach Widdel*, means 'Brynach the Irishman'. Another twelve churches are dedicated to him, situated along the ancient routes from Brecon to Ireland, concentrated at their western end, near the embarkation points for Ireland. His church in Nevern is at the foot of one of the best-preserved Iron Age hill forts in Wales. Built on the slopes of Mynydd Carningli, the crumbling walls and towers of the stronghold dominate the village of Nevern. Inscribed stones dating from the fifth or sixth century indicate that Nevern was an early monastic site, while its elaborate tenth- or eleventh-century cross suggests that it continued to play a significant role in Pembrokeshire.

There are two fifth-century gravestones at the site with inscriptions both in Latin and in Irish ogham. This is a cipher which uses the sound-values of spoken Latin, and consists of incised lines grouped along two adjacent sides of a stone slab; stonemasons found it easier to cut simple strokes than to carve the rounded letters of the Latin alphabet. The use of ogham in Wales indicates links with southern Ireland in the early medieval period. Some memorial stones inscribed in Latin or in ogham are found in the north-west, but most are in south-west Wales (particularly in Pembrokeshire), with further clusters in Brecon and Glamorgan.

In the Henllys Chapel in the south transept of Nevern church, two inscribed stones are set into the window sills. One bilingual gravestone dates from the fifth or early sixth century. Its Latin inscription, 'MAGLOCUNI FILI CLUTORI', is repeated in ogham and means: '[the monument] of Maglocunus [or Maelgwyn in Welsh], son of Clutorius'. On a nearby windowsill, a much later tombstone probably dates from the tenth century. It is decorated with an interlaced Latin cross, carved in low relief (see photo below). Perhaps unintentionally, it resembles a human figure; this is a characteristic Irish form of cross.

Outside the church to the east of the porch, a bilingual stone, 5 feet tall, dates from around AD 500 and commemorates a Christian named Vitalianus in both Latin and

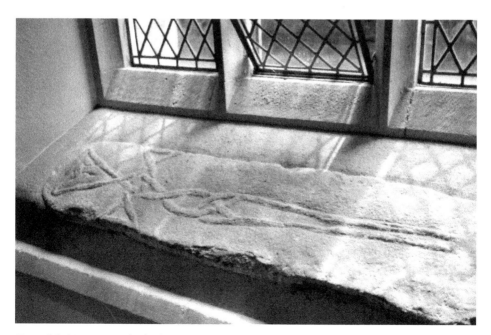

Cross slab, Nevern, Pembrokeshire.

High cross, Nevern, Pembrokeshire.

ogham. It is inscribed in Latin 'VITALIANI EMERTO'; Vitalianus and Emeritus, perhaps meaning 'worthy of honour', were common names at this time.

Nearby stands a great wheel-headed cross, 4 metres high, carved in the late tenth or early eleventh century and covered with elaborate knotwork panels; it is one of the finest in Wales. Wheel-headed slab crosses are mainly found in Pembrokeshire, at Penally, Carew, and Nevern, for example; they resemble examples in Northumbria.

The cross at Nevern consists of two sections, the upper wheel-head being attached to the shouldered neck by a mortise and tenon joint. Both slabs are cut from local dolerite stone, a hard volcanic rock which is difficult to carve. The Stonehenge bluestones are formed of dolerite that is likely to have come from the Preseli Hills above Nevern. Set into the braided decoration of the high cross, a small panel on one side reads DNS—an abbreviated form of *Dominus* (Latin for 'The Lord')—while a panel on the opposite face, of uncertain meaning, reads 'H/AN/.EH'.

The Life of Brynach

According to the author of his twelfth-century Life, Brynach travelled from an unknown place (probably Ireland) to Rome and Brittany, and landed at Milford Haven on the Pembrokeshire coast. He built various oratories near the rivers Cleddau, Gwaun, and Caman, and at the foot of Mynydd Carningli. Brynach was the chaplain, or 'soul-friend' of Brychan, the legendary ruler of Brecon, and married one of his daughters.

A chieftain named Clether gave Brynach land for a church at Nevern, with the Caman Brook as a boundary between them. Clether then retired to Cornwall and lived as a hermit at a site now named St Clether, at the foot of Bodmin Moor. Brynach was harassed by King Maelgwyn of Gwynedd for a while, until he wrought miracles and the two came to terms; this recalls the early tombstone inscribed to a Christian named Maelgwyn in Nevern church. The author adds touches of humour unusual in saints' Lives in his descriptions of Brynach's adventures.

Episodes in Brynach's Life are linked with local sites in order to explain their origin, as one often finds in medieval saints' Lives. Thus the well in which Brynach washed off blood from a wound (*Life*, ch. 4) is called *Fons Rubeus* (or 'red well'); it was still known when his Life was written. We are told that through Brynach, the well now heals others; it is a place 'where also in honour of the saint the merciful God bestows many benefits of health on the infirm, the healing of wounds through mediation of the Lord being received without delay'.[16] A chalybeate spring naturally stains water red.

The Life explains the origin of churches named after Brynach; he is said to have driven out evil spirits at Pontfaen (ch. 5), where a church is dedicated to him, with two carved stone crosses dating from the ninth to the eleventh centuries. Brynach has visions of angels, which are linked to the nearby mountain of Mynydd Carningl—*ingli* meaning 'angels' (ch. 9). An oak tree is named 'Bread Oak' on account of a miracle that he performs (ch. 14)—when Brynach had no food, he picked loaves from the oak's branches.[17]

The author tells us that in later life Brynach became a hermit in the mountains above Nevern, from where Ireland can be seen on a clear day. He died and was buried beneath the eastern wall of his church at Nevern (ch. 16). The Life thus perpetuates and consolidates oral traditions concerning Brynach; it connects the monastic community at Nevern with the surrounding landscape, and justifies its territorial claims.

A Wild Boar

Brynach's Life relates how a white sow shows him where to build his monastery:

> On the following night, while St Brynach was prostrate in prayer, an angel of the Lord appeared, saying, 'This place is not the place of your dwelling, but go along the river bank as far as the second stream which flows into the river, and watch the bank of that stream until you see a wild white sow with white piglets, and there build for yourself a fixed habitation'. Therefore the saint proceeding, gladdened by the angelic message, found the promised sow, with her piglets in the place, where in his name a church, having been built, is now served on the bank of the Caman Brook.[18]

A wild boar quite often features in the story of a Celtic monk's chief foundation; the pig acts as an instrument of God's will, showing the saint where to build. For Celtic peoples, pigs grazing the woodland were a main source of food. Domesday Book (1086) measured woodland in terms of the number of swine it could support, acorns forming an important part of their diet.

Swineherds worked on the edge of settlements, where their pigs could forage in the forest or in the wilderness, and where a monk could find a 'desert place' in order to seek God. Both monks and swineherds interacted between wild and settled places; saints went into the wilderness, which swineherds knew about. Pigs roam in search of mast, and they could lead saints to unclaimed territory. Swine appear in a surprising number of saints' Lives: six from Ireland (Ciarán of Saighir, Rúadán, Mochoemóc, Fínán, Fíacc, and Finnian of Clonard), four from Wales (Cadog, Brynach, Dyfrig, and Illtud), two from Brittany (Paul Aurélien and Malo), one from Scotland (Kentigern), and one from Somerset (Cyngar). The earliest of these is the late eleventh-century *Life of St Cadog* by Lifris of Llancarfan, in south-east Wales.[19] The pig foundation tales belong to pseudo-history. Typically, a saint who has been granted a tract of land looks for the best site on which to build a church; an angel appears in a vision and explains that a pig will show him the site. On the next day, the saint sees the pig, which marks the spot.

When a monk searched for the place where he would live and die, and which would become the place of his resurrection, the appearance of a wild boar came to symbolise God's approval of the site. Readers familiar with the classics would remember that in Virgil's *Aeneid* a huge white sow showed Ascanius where to found the great city of Alba Longa, the precursor of Rome.[20] There were many pig tales in non-religious Celtic literature, such as the Fourth Branch of the Mabinogion.[21] The boar was also an ancient Celtic symbol of power and authority; it was portrayed on regalia, cauldrons, and rock carvings. It could therefore be seen to symbolise both God's power and the authority of a saint.

Llanwnda

Nine miles west of Nevern, a large parish is named after a local saint, Degan. There is an extraordinary range of early medieval sculpture at the site, including five crosses now built into the outer wall of the small church. They were perhaps carved locally in the ninth to the eleventh centuries, and display possible Viking influence.[22] The site is 10 miles north-east of St David's, on a clifftop above present-day Fishguard, close to a crossing point for Ireland.

The church is named after a reputed disciple of St David named Gwynda. Two local stories of unknown date convey later attitudes to these early saints. In the first, Gwynda travelled westwards with Áedán, another monk, to St David's. When they were 2 miles from their destination, they stopped to drink at a well, Ffynnon Tregroes (or 'well at the village crossroads') in Whitchurch parish. Each wished to give his name to the well, so they fought and Gwynda lost. Áedán named the well after himself and continued to St David's, while Gwynda went on to Llanwnda.[23]

In another story, at the boundary stream of Llanwnda, Gwynda's horse reared at a jumping fish. Gwynda fell off and cursed the water, which is why there are no fish in the stream that springs from his holy well (see colour plate 6). The story shows a typically Welsh approach to blessing and cursing.

Gerald of Wales (*c.* 1146–1223) was the incumbent at Llanwnda for a time; he was author of *A Journey through Wales* (*Itinerarium Kambriae*), *A Description of Wales* (*Descriptio*

Kambriae), and a Life of David that was a shortened version of Rhygyfarch's. Gerald was a canon at St David's, archdeacon of Brecon, and an unsuccessful candidate for the bishopric of St David's. He accompanied Archbishop Baldwin of Canterbury on his journey around Wales in 1188 to enlist support for the Third Crusade, which Gerald vowed to join, but he was subsequently released from his vow because of his age and poor health, on condition that 'he gave work and aid to the repair of the church of Menevia'.[24]

Teilo of Llandeilo Fawr

Teilo was an early monk whose cult was centred on Llandeilo Fawr, above the River Tywi in south Wales. His name is of a type found in sixth-century Ireland and Britain, and there are some early written references to the monastery that bears his name. In about 1130, Geoffrey of Llandaf wrote a biographical sermon about Teilo, linking him with famous Celtic monks in order to promote Llandaf's territorial claims.

The extent of the early monastery at Llandeilo Fawr is outlined by the very large churchyard of 3.5 acres. It is bisected by the town's main street, which may follow the line of a Roman road. A spring rises near the east end of the church, and flows into a large chamber beneath it. This may be the site of a baptistry in which converts were immersed. The spring provided the town with its water until the nineteenth century; today it bubbles into an alcove on the outside of the churchyard wall.

Llandeilo Fawr became an important bishop's seat, but it is not known when this happened. There was an earlier 'bishop-house' of Dyfed at *Llan Teulydawc*, which was probably the Priory of St John and St Teulyddog at Carmarthen, downstream from Landeilo Fawr. This bishop-house may have been eclipsed by Llandeilo Fawr in the seventh or eighth century; a ninth-century marginal inscription in the Lichfield Gospels contains the phrase *Nobis episcopus Teiliau*, referring to the bishop of Llandeilo Fawr.[25] Teilo's cult became popular in south Wales—thirty-three churches are named after him.

The heads of two finely carved high crosses from the ninth century indicate the importance of the monastery; on one is an equal-armed cross, covered in a carved interlace pattern, while the other is decorated with circles that recall both prehistoric cup-and-ring marks and contemporary embossed metalwork. Their designs are different from those found on crosses near the Pembrokeshire coast, which suggests that there were regional workshops associated with the chief monasteries.[26]

The Lichfield Gospels

At some point, the monastery of Llandeilo Fawr was given a magnificent Irish or Mercian gospel book now known as the Lichfield (or St Chad) Gospels; it is the earliest surviving gospel book known to have been used in Wales. The book was created in the eighth or ninth century, and is written in an Insular, half-uncial hand. The gospel book was perhaps paid as tribute to a Saxon king, for some time after 850 it was in the ownership of St Chad's cathedral,

Above left: St Teilo's well, Llandeilo Fawr, Carmarthenshire.

Above right: Ornamented cross head, Llandeilo Fawr, Carmarthenshire.

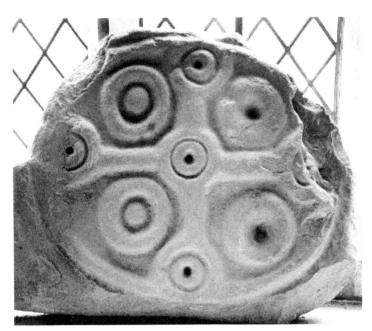

Circular cross head, Llandeilo Fawr, Carmarthenshire.

Lichfield, where it still remains. It was at Lichfield Cathedral by the early eleventh century, for it contains a reference to Leofric, who was bishop of Lichfield from 1020 to 1026.

While the gospel book was in Wales, monks wrote entries in Welsh in its margins, recording gifts to the bishop of Llandeilo Fawr. These records of land transactions and legal settlements, most of which closely resemble charters, are some of the earliest surviving examples of written Welsh. A marginal annotation at the end of St Matthew's gospel informs us about the history of the book; it was given to the monastery at Llandeilo Fawr 'for the good of his soul' by a man named Gelhi, who had bought the book from a certain Cingal in exchange for his best horse:

> Here it is shown that Gelhi, son of Arihtiud, bought this Gospel from Cingal, and gave him for it his best horse and gave for the sake of his soul this Gospel to God and St Teilo upon the altar.[27]

The 'altar of St Teilo' is generally thought to refer to the monastery church at Llandeilo Fawr. An earlier addition to the same page records that before Gelhi gave the book to the church there was a court action in which one Tutbulc accused Gelhi and his family of corruption. Since there was still space left unfilled on the page at the end of Matthew's gospel, a Saxon filled most of the remainder with a list of Anglo-Saxon personal names.[28] Some of the marginal notes in the Lichfield Gospels, such as the group known as 'Chad 8', appear to be records of the names of people prayed for during the liturgy.

The manuscript resembles gospel books produced in Northumbria and Ireland—the Lindisfarne Gospels, the Book of Kells, and the Book of Durrow. However, the pigmentation of some of the illustrations in the Lichfield Gospels resembles the colour scheme on an eighth-century carved stone angel believed to have been part of the shrine of St Chad at Lichfield, so the book may have been decorated at Lichfield and taken to Wales in the 870s, when Viking raiders sacked Lichfield. If so, the gospel book was later returned.[29]

The manuscript contains eight decorated pages, including full-page portraits of two of the evangelists; St Luke holds a pastoral staff modelled on those carried by abbots of the Near East (see front cover photo). There is a page of intricate eastern-style 'carpet' decoration, in which fish, dogs, and pelicans are intertwined. Each gospel begins with an elaborate initial letter, and a page depicts the four evangelists as the four beasts in the Book of Revelation (Rev. 4. 6–8), enclosed within an elaborate frame.

A gospel book at Hereford Cathedral resembles the Lichfield Gospels both in its text and in the decoration of its initials; the structure and text of the Hereford Gospels suggest that it was created in Wales in the eighth or early ninth century.[30] It probably came to Hereford in the early eleventh century. Although few early Welsh manuscripts survive, they are likely to have existed, for their influence on stone sculpture can be seen in stonemasons' use of half-uncial script and geometric capitals. Monastic stonemasons also demonstrated their knowledge of manuscripts in the layout, phrasing, and vocabulary found on inscribed stones, and in the abbreviations and contractions which they employed, as we have already seen.[31]

Civil Transactions

Gospel books were not only revered as relics; they also represented God's presence as a witness to such civil transactions as grants of land; these were recorded 'in God's presence' by being inscribed in the margins of the gospel book. The earliest surviving examples of this practice occur in the Lichfield Gospels, with records of the settlement of land-disputes between two individuals being deposited with the community of St Teilo and inserted in the gospel book.[32]

We catch a glimpse of how this happened from an account in the Hereford Gospels during the reign of King Cnut (990–1035), when Leofflæd, the wife of Thorkil the White, was given the right to some land. The text concludes: 'Then Thorkil rode to St Æthelbert's Minster [Hereford Cathedral], with the consent and cognisance of the whole assembly, and had it recorded in the gospel book.'[33]

Brechfa, 5 miles north of the Carmarthen-Llandeilo road, is also dedicated to St Teilo. A marginal note in the Lichfield Gospels describes how it was gifted to the monastery at Llandeilo Fawr:

> This writing shows that Rhys and Hirv [gave to God and St Teilo] Brechfa as far as Hirvaen Gwyddog, from the desert of Gelli Irlath as far as Camddwr. Its rent payment is 60 loaves, and a wether sheep, and a quantity of butter…

The church at Brechfa has been heavily restored; the stone surround of St Teilo's well can be seen opposite the church, in Victoria Park, on the bank of the River Marlais, a tributary of the Towy. The well is now dry.

St Teilo's well, Brechfa, Carmarthenshire.

Early Leaders at Llanilltud Fawr: Samson, Illtud and Dyfrig

We learn about Llanilltud Fawr in a long and interesting Life of Samson (*c.* 490–*c.* 565) written by a Breton monk, perhaps as early as the first quarter of the seventh century. The author also refers to Illtud and Dyfrig (or Dubricius in Latin), providing us with the earliest information we possess concerning these leaders of the Welsh Church. All three monks were active at the monastery of Llanilltud Fawr in south-east Wales, and they were also involved with its daughter house on Caldey Island, off the Pembrokeshire coast, 40 ? miles to the west.

The *Life of Samson*

In its plain and direct Latin style, this work is very different from Welsh saints' Lives of the eleventh century and later, with their concern to present their subjects interacting with kings and princes, and their intention to confirm his community's territorial claims. Samson's Life also reflects the primitive monasticism found in the *Lives of the Desert Fathers*: it describes Samson's asceticism and his constant search for solitude. At the same time, he is depicted as being gentle and considerate to others.

In the prologue, the author explains that his source of information is a monk who lived for many years in a British monastery founded by Samson, and who now, as an old man, has come to live in the same community as the author. The elderly monk had an uncle named Henoc, who was a cousin of Samson and who often talked about him. The authors of later saints' Lives often claim to base their work on early sources, but their claims are frequently dubious. However, the author of Samson's Life is possibly accurate when he says:

> These words … I derived from a certain religious and venerable old man whose house beyond the sea Samson himself had founded. He led a catholic and religious life there for nearly eighty years. In times most approximate to those of the aforesaid St Samson, the mother of St Samson reported these deeds to his uncle [Henoc], a very holy deacon, himself the cousin of St Samson; of what follows [the venerable old man] assured me truthfully, relating to me many parts of the saint's wonderful career.

And not only so, but there are also very many and delightful accounts of the amazing deeds which he performed ... which were written in suitably elegant style and taken across the sea by the said holy deacon, Henoc by name. The venerable old man, of whom we have already spoken, who lived in this monastery, caused them continually to be read piously and attentively before me.[1]

Supernatural Elements in the *Life*

The author begins in a style typical of later saints' Lives, by demonstrating Samson's holiness through using phrases from the gospels. In Luke's Gospel, Elizabeth is barren until an angel tells her husband that she will give birth to John the Baptist, who will be a great prophet (Luke 1. 5–25). Similarly, in the *Life of Samson*, his mother Anna was thought barren until she was told in a dream of the future birth of her child and of his priestly vocation. In the dream she is told, 'Blessed is your womb and more blessed is the fruit of your womb.' This recalls Elizabeth's greeting to the Virgin Mary (Luke. 1. 42).

Jesus heals the sick, casts out devils and raises a widow's son to life (Luke. 7. 11–17). In the same way, Samson's power is demonstrated by healing the sick, casting out devils, and raising a dead boy to life. St Luke relates that at Pentecost, tongues of fire came down on the disciples, who were then empowered to go and preach (Acts 2. 1–4). There is an echo of this in Samson's Life, when its author writes that after his consecration as a bishop, fire came from Samson's mouth and nostrils. This demonstrates Samson's power over the elements, a quality attributed to Christ in the Gospels and also, in some medieval Welsh texts, to magicians.

At other points in the Life, the author praises what appear to be druidic powers of Christian monks. We are told that Illtud, with whom Samson studied, was 'by birth a most learned magician (*magicus*), having knowledge of the future'. Some early copyists were uncomfortable with the term *magicus* and altered the word to *magnificus* (or 'noble').[2] The author describes how Samson tames a witch who brandishes a 'bloody trident', and how he kills a large serpent. Snakes are often killed by early Christian saints, while Patrick was said to have banished snakes from Ireland. In addition to its biblical associations with the fall of Adam and Eve, a serpent could represent a pagan deity vanquished by God's power.[3]

St Illtud's Monastery

The Life relates that Samson's parents took the youngster to the monastery of Llanilltud Fawr (or 'Illtud's great church'):

...to the school of the famous master of the Britons, Eltut [Illtud] by name. Now this Eltut was a disciple of St Germanus [of Auxerre, d. *c.* 448], and St Germanus himself had ordained [Eltut] in his youth. And in truth Eltut was of all the Britons the most accomplished in the Scriptures, namely of the Old and New Testaments, and in philosophy of every kind, of form, geometry namely, and of rhetoric, grammar and arithmetic, and of all the theories of philosophy. And by birth he was a most wise magician, having knowledge of the future.[4]

The writer adds a personal comment: 'I have been in his magnificent monastery'. Illtud was a renowned teacher: his education was not only monastic but Roman, and its emphasis on philosophy, rhetoric, and mathematics perhaps hints that a classical education continued in some form after the Roman infrastructure had collapsed.

Llanilltud Fawr (in English, Llantwit Major) is on the south coast of Wales, in the Vale of Glamorgan, 9 miles west of Barry. It is hidden in a small river valley, where it would have been out of the sight of pirates; nearby St Donats provided a natural harbour. This became the most influential early Welsh monastery—Gildas and Paulinus (see Chapter 5) were said to have studied here, as well as Samson.

The author of the *Life of Samson* depicts a tender relationship between Abbot Illtud and the teenager:

When [Samson] was about fifteen he exercised himself in the very frequent fasts and the longer vigils which were kept by all the brothers who lived there, so much so … that that most sensible master forbade him and said to him, 'It is not meet, little son, that the tender body of a youth, up till now in the flowering stage, should be broken by too many and ill-regulated fasts'.[5]

The Life relates that Bishop Dyfrig came to Illtud's monastery to ordain two presbyters, and to ordain Samson as a deacon. When Samson had lived for some time in the large community at Llanilltud Fawr, he longed for greater solitude, and wondered how to achieve this without upsetting Abbot Illtud. God kindly arranged for an angel to tell the abbot to ask Samson what he desired. After doing so, Illtud sent him to Ynys Pyr, which is almost certainly Caldey Island, where Samson could now lead a more solitary life, 'with untiring patience a wonderful, isolated and above all a heavenly life', under the direction of a holy man named Pyr:

[Samson] ceased not, day or night, from prayer and communion with God. Spending the whole day in working with his hands and in prayer, and the whole night, moreover, in mystical interpretation of the Holy Scriptures, he carried the lamp to his dwelling in order that, bent upon reading, he might either write something or exercise himself in spiritual contemplation; for though, as a man, he had need of rest for the sake of human weakness and reclined against the wall or anything hard for support, he never slept in a bed.[6]

The Life's account of Samson's radical asceticism reflects the influence of Cassian and the Desert Fathers. Antony of Egypt (*c.* 250–356) left his community to live alone with God, just as Samson lived alone on Caldey Island and later in a cave beside the River Severn (ch. 41). Impressed by his holiness, the elderly bishop Dyfrig then appointed Samson as cellarer (or bursar of the community) on Caldey Island. This task required wisdom, because a cellarer had influence over the lifestyle of the monks—including their food and drink, and their gifts to the poor. We are told:

> Knowing that St Samson was endowed by God, in that hour [Bishop Dyfrig] bestowed upon him the office of cellarer, saying to him, 'I ordain and above all I desire in the Lord that all the goods which abound in this storehouse by the gift of God shall be administered and shared by you'. Thereupon, acting in accordance with the old man's bidding, for the sake of obedience, he did all things according to God; for at every moment he seemed to dispense everything in the name of God and of charity.[7]

Caldey Island

One can perhaps gain the clearest impression of how Samson lived by taking a boat to Caldey Island, which is 2 miles south of Tenby, at the south-western point of Cardigan Bay. There are frequent daily boat crossings on weekdays throughout the year; the journey takes about twenty minutes. There are Saturday sailings from mid-May to mid-September, but none on Sundays. This enables the Cistercian monks who now live on the island to enjoy its tranquillity once a week. At high tide, boats leave from Tenby harbour; at low water, they depart from the landing stage on Castle Beach.

Samson's Life calls the island Ynys Pyr after its first abbot. The author describes Pyr's undignified death: walking back to his cell one night, the drunken abbot fell into the monastery's well and drowned (ch. 36). Bishop Dyfrig appointed Samson as abbot to replace Pyr:

> One dark night … Pyr took a solitary stroll into the grounds of the monastery, and what is more serious, so it is said, owing to stupid intoxication, fell headlong into a deep pit. Uttering one piercing cry for help, he was dragged out of the hole by the brothers in a dying condition, and died in the night from his adventure.
>
> And it came to pass when the bishop heard of it, he made all the brothers to remain just where they were and spend the night together; and then, having assembled a council, after Matins, all the men of this monastery, with one accord, chose St Samson to be abbot.… He trained the brothers gently to the proper rule.[8]

There are many caves around the island's coastline: the monks may have lived in these, and in wattle huts clustered around a church, near the spring that still supplies the island with abundant fresh water. Linked with the monastery, at some point there was a community of nuns on St Margaret's Island, which is close to Caldey. At that time it was possible to walk across low-lying marsh to St Margaret's Island from the mainland at Penally.

Caldey was a foundation of some significance; a piece of sixth-century imported Mediterranean tableware from the Byzantine Empire was found in the New Orchard near St David's chapel on Caldey, and more fragments were found on the mainland. The base of a seventh-century jar from Gaul was also found near St David's chapel. Many cist (or slab-lined) graves were found here, indicating an early medieval cemetery. Here, where there are dunes, to the east of the present jetty, the tide came in almost up to the chapel (see colour plate 3), which was named after St David only in the nineteenth century.

Near the centre of the island is St Illtud's church and the remains of a Norman priory, with a distinctive stone watchtower. The priory has a well-preserved twelfth- to fifteenth-century cloister garth. This was a small, working monastic cloister near the only water supply on the island. The spring is due to a fault between the Old Red Sandstone to the north and the Carboniferous Limestone to the south. The present church, with its floor of cobble stones, dates from the thirteenth and fourteenth centuries.

Located against the south wall of the nave is a grave slab, broadly dating from Samson's time. It is inscribed in ogham 'Magl Dubr…' which has been interpreted as perhaps meaning '(the stone of) the tonsured servant of Dubricius'. It also bears a Latin inscription. The translation of its opening lines is uncertain, but it continues: 'I ask all who walk in this place to pray for the soul of Cadwgan'. Its use of half-uncial script (the word uncial means 'an inch') shows that the stonemason was familiar with early manuscripts. The grave slab was found in a field near the farm, in which there was another early cemetery; writing in about 1811, the antiquarian Fenton says that the stone was dug up 'many years ago'.

St Illtud's church, with its cobbled floor, Caldey Island.

Ogham-inscribed stone, St Illtud's church, Caldey Island.

The priory was established by Tyronensian monks from St Dogmaels, close to Cardigan, 30 miles to the north and near the mouth of the River Teifi. St Dogmaels was founded in 1118; its motherhouse was at Tyron, in France. Like the Cistercians, the Tyronensians were an early reform of the Benedictine order, following the tradition of the Desert Fathers with a renewed emphasis on labour and a vegetarian diet. Caldey was by then a very poor monastery, perhaps a small cell of St Dogmaels.

Samson Retires to a Cave

On a visit to Ireland, Samson acquired a chariot, or light cart, in which to travel. After only eighteen months as abbot of Caldey, Samson then withdrew to a quieter place, a ruined fort near the Welsh bank of the River Severn, with his father Amon and two companions:

> And he caused Amon to come with him … four of them altogether, to a very desolate wilderness, and, having discovered a very delightful fort near the River Severn, and in it a spring of very sweet water, he set about making a dwelling for his brothers, while he prayed that the Lord would be pleased to show him some underground cave and the Lord graciously fulfilled that most faithful prayer.
>
> For, on a certain day, as he wandered through the forest he found a very spacious and very lonely cave, and its mouth being situated towards the east, he embraced it affectionately as though it had been given by God for a dwelling. … and up to the time when I was in Britain the place, in which the three before-mentioned brothers were, was always revered with great devotion, and also an oratory constructed therein, where St Samson was wont to come every Sunday to sing Mass and for Christ's communion.[9]

When Samson prayed that God would show him a cave, he was following an ancient Jewish and Christian tradition. The Book of Exodus in the Old Testament relates that God showed his glory to Moses in a cave at the top of Mount Sinai (Exodus 33. 18–23), and the Prophet Elijah was said to have climbed to the same cave in order to meet God (1 Kings 19. 9–13). Pilgrims to the Holy Land knew that Jesus was born in a cave at Bethlehem, and buried in a cave outside Jerusalem.

In early times, a cave provided a simple yet practical hermitage—warm in winter and cool in summer. Hermitages are often described in saints' Lives, and a number of caves around the Welsh coast are associated with early monks. Hermitages are difficult to date archaeologically, but their existence is often described in twelfth-century Lives of saints.

Llanilltud Fawr

The Life implies that Samson's former abbot, Illtud, died in his monastery at Llanilltud Fawr. After enjoying his time of retreat in the cave, Samson returned to community life and became abbot of Llanilltud Fawr at the request of a synod. When his brother monks brought

Samson to attend the synod, his face was 'radiant, like that of an angel', just as Antony of Egypt emerged radiant from his fort when his friends found him after twenty years:

> His friends broke the door down by force. Antony came out … radiant as though from some shrine where he had been led into divine mysteries and inspired by God.[10]

We are told of Samson:

> He came, though not with willing steps, to the synod with them. … But when the elders saw him with a countenance exceedingly joyful, as if they beheld an angel of God, they received St Samson with reverent greeting and appointed him abbot against his will.[11]

Today there are two late medieval churches at Llanilltud Fawr, built end-to-end. The Celtic church probably stood on the site of the present west church, which now contains a fine collection of monuments from early times: they commemorate abbots and kings, and indicate the continuing importance of Illtud's monastery. There may have been a burial chapel containing the grave of Illtud at the site.[12] The twelfth-century *Brut y Tywysogion* (or *Chronicle of the Princes*) relates that Vikings destroyed Llanilltud Fawr during raids in the later tenth century.

One of the earliest monuments at Llanilltud Fawr, the Samson Cross, refers not to St Samson but to a later king with the same name; it dates from the late ninth or early tenth century. Its shaft, which was probably once capped by a wheel cross, contains two

Crosses of Samson and Houelt, Llanilltud Fawr, Glamorgan.

Latin inscriptions in three pairs of panels, which perhaps represent open books or even wax tablets, which were used for a range of purposes—such as learning to read or write. The paired panels on its east face, which can be seen in the photo on p. 61, read: '+Samson placed this cross for his soul', while the two pairs of panels on its west face read: '[for the souls of] Illtud, Samson the king' and '[for the souls of] Samuel [and] Ebisar'. It appears that King Samson erected the cross before his death, to commemorate himself in advance.[13]

To the right, behind the Samson cross, in the same photograph, is a cross with a circular head, carved from local gritstone at the command of King Houelt in the late ninth century. At the base of the cross is an inscription in Latin half-uncial script: 'In the name of God the Father and the Holy Spirit. Houelt prepared this cross for the soul of Res, his father'. Houelt was probably Hywel ap Rhys, King of Glywysing, a region between Swansea and Newport. Hywel was a subject of King Alfred of Wessex in 884, and died in the following year, according to the *Chronicle of the Princes*.[14]

Much of the surface of the cross is magnificently decorated with shallow triangular key-patterns, which recall motifs found in illuminated manuscripts. Both the inscription and the style of decoration resemble examples of the same date in Ireland. This suggests that the Houelt cross may have been the work of an Irish sculptor, or of one trained in Ireland.[15]

Another slab, the Pillar of Samson, on the right in the photo on page 63, reads:

> In the name of God most High begins the cross of the Saviour, which Abbot Samson prepared for his own soul and for the soul of King Juthahel and [for the souls] of Artmail and Tecain.

The king commemorated on the pillar might be Iudhail, King of Gwent, who died in about 848. This may be the monument that the twelfth-century *Life of Illtud* erroneously describes St Samson erecting in his own memory (ch. 15).[16]

Samson Leaves Llanilltud Fawr

According to Samson's Life, one Easter night, while he was praying alone in the church at Llanilltud Fawr, an angel appeared in a vision, telling him to leave the monastery and set out across the sea as a pilgrim. The angel said:

> 'I have been sent to you by my Lord; of a truth you ought to tarry no longer in this country, for you are ordained to be a pilgrim, and beyond the sea you will be very great in the Church and worthy of the highest priestly dignity.' ...
>
> On the arrival of the brothers for the morning chapter, the angel gently withdrew and left; and [Samson], accepting the omen with all the eagerness of faith and keeping it carefully in his mind, when he had finished the office of the Paschal Celebration, forthwith, amid the regrets and tears of the whole congregation, directed his course towards this side of the Severn Sea.[17]

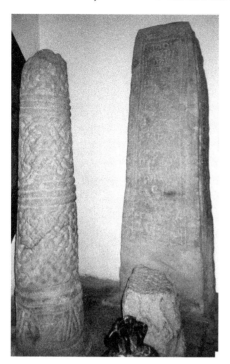 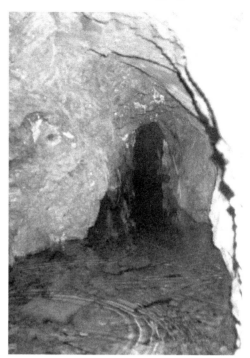

Above left: Pillars of Samson and Illtud, Llanilltud Fawr, Glamorgan.

Above right: St Samson's cave, Golant, near Fowey, Cornwall.

Samson set sail for Cornwall with a group of relatives, landing at Padstow and continuing up the Camel estuary until they came within 2 miles of the monastery of Docco (ch. 45), now named St Kew. They hoped to break their journey there, but the community sent one of their number, Juniavus, to dissuade Samson from doing so, since the monastery had grown lax (ch. 46). Samson and his friends continued southwards across Cornwall. As they travelled, they met a group of people with their chieftain, 'celebrating the mysteries of their ancestors'. Samson carved a cross on a standing stone, and healed a boy who had fallen unconscious from his horse.

The ruler told his followers to come forward and reaffirm their baptism. He next asked Samson to drive an evil serpent from a cave, which the monk did. According to tradition, the cave can still be seen at Golant, 2 miles north of Fowey, where a church and holy well are named after Samson. After he had killed the serpent, the grateful chief and his followers asked Samson to become their bishop. He refused, but accepted the offer of the cave as a retreat (ch. 50). Samson's cave can be seen at Golant, down by the harbour. It is beside the railway, behind the third telegraph pole alongside the track. It is a long cavern, and it can be explored with wellingtons and a torch (see photo above).

Samson in Brittany

Samson established a monastery, perhaps at Fowey, leaving his father Amon in charge of the new community; he then sailed to Brittany with his followers. He founded Dol on the north coast, and several other monasteries. He signed decrees of Church Councils in Paris in 553 and 557. On one of his journeys to Paris, a wheel fell off his much-used chariot. Samson took an active part in Breton politics, and has dedications in eastern Brittany and Normandy. A town in Guernsey and one of the Scilly Isles are named after him.

The author of Samson's Life describes him primarily as a monk who happened to become abbot of Dol. By contrast, a later *Life of Samson*, written at Dol in about 850 by a Benedictine monk, portrays him as a ninth-century bishop, since the monastery had just been proclaimed a bishopric at the synod of Coetleu in 848–9. This Life was in turn re-written in about 1124 by the archbishop of Dol, Baudri de Bourgueil, who presents Samson as an eleventh-century wandering preacher and a hermit. At this time there was a struggle for supremacy between Tours and Dol, so Baudri takes care to emphasise that the archbishopric was conferred 'not only on St Samson but also on his successor' (ch. 24).[18]

Bishop Dyfrig

We know a little about Dyfrig because he features in the *Life of Samson*. Dyfrig is presented as a prominent figure among the Christians of south Wales at the end of the sixth century. He was perhaps the equivalent of a later archbishop, his authority extending over more than one kingdom. As we have seen, Dyfrig appointed Samson as abbot of the community on what was probably Caldey Island, 2 miles south of Tenby; he therefore appears to have exercised a ministry within both Glamorgan and Pembrokeshire. It has been suggested that he was based in the former Roman town of Caerwent, although this perhaps assumes that he lived according to an earlier, Roman, model of bishop.[19]

Dyfrig was later associated with the territory of Ergyng in south-west Herefordshire, but this appears to be related to an attempt by the diocese of Llandaf to assert its authority in the region of the Welsh Borders, where the bishops of both St David's and Llandaf were attempting to develop their sphere of influence. In the twelfth century, the Norman bishop Urban of Llandaf began the compilation of the *Liber Landavensis*, or *Book of Llandaf*. This contains a collection of saints' Lives, papal bulls, and charters which are claimed to date from the sixth to the eleventh century; while some of these are likely to be based on earlier sources, others are of more dubious origin, being intended to justify Llandaf's territorial claims and consolidate its power at a time when the Normans were gaining control over Wales.[20]

According to his twelfth-century Life in the *Book of Llandaf*, Dyfrig was born at Madley, near Hereford, his mother being the daughter of Pepiau, a chieftain of Ergyng. The Life relates that finding his daughter pregnant, he had her put into a sack and thrown into the nearby River Wye. When she was washed onto a sand bank, he ordered her to be burnt, but the next morning she was found on the pyre, nursing Dyfrig. When Pepiau let the child stroke his cheeks, the baby cured him of dribbling.

A church beside the River Wye at Whitchurch, 4 miles north-east of Monmouth, is dedicated to Dyfrig. Whitchurch means 'white' or 'stone' church, and denotes a more substantial and imposing construction at a time when most churches were built of wood. There is a fine twelfth-century font in the church, decorated with arcading, and a landing stage in the churchyard, enabling churchgoers to arrive by boat.

Rivers were an important means of travel in Celtic times, when much of the land was forest, mountain, or marsh. Some Roman roads survived, strongly built for troops to march along, but these gradually fell into ruin. River travel was by coracle: this was a light, circular craft, constructed of hide stretched over a wicker frame. The style of construction and type of wood differed in each locality, depending on the speed of the river and the types of material available. Even today, Welsh coracle men are skilled at using coracles for a range of activities—from fishing to dipping sheep and salmon poaching—as well as for transport.

Hentland

Dyfrig's Life in the *Book of Llandaf* relates that his chief monastery was at Hentland. There was a Roman building on the site, which is at the end of a road half a mile south of Kynaston, 4 miles west-north-west of Ross-on-Wye.[21] The name of this church derives from *hen llan*, meaning 'old, or former, church'; it can refer to a church which was restored

Above left: Ancient landing stage on the Wye, Whitchurch, Hereford and Worcester.

Above right: St Dyfrig's church, Hentland, Hereford and Worcester.

after a period of disuse.[25] Part of its nave dates from 1050, but most of the church is thirteenth-century. There is a fine lantern cross on its original base in the churchyard, also dating from the thirteenth century; its worn carvings include a crucifixion and a carving of a Dyfrig as a mitred bishop (see photo on previous page).

There may have been a second church in the cemetery at Hentland dedicated to St Teilo. One of the Llandaf charters lists the churches consecrated by Bishop Herewald (1056–1104), the predecessor of Bishop Urban. The charter states:

> In the time of Edward, King of England, and Gruffydd, King of Wales, Bishop Herewald consecrated [at] Henllan [a church to] Dyfrig and Llandeilo in one churchyard.

> *Tempore Erguardi Regis Angliae et Grifudi Regis Gualiae consecrauit Hergualdis episcopus Henllan Dibric et Lann Teliau in uno cimiterio.*

It is unclear whether the bishop was consecrating newly-built churches or re-consecrating those which had been damaged earlier, perhaps following the raids of Gruffydd ap Llywelyn in the area. The latter is perhaps more likely; it might also explain the name *Hen llan*, or 'former church'.[22]

Moccas

The twelfth-century *Life of Dyfrig* relates that after he spent seven years in the monastery at Hentland, he founded a church at Moccas, which is 8 miles east of Hay-on-Wye and a mile north of Blakemere. We are told that a white sow showed Dyfrig where to build his church at Moccas, referring to the meaning of its name, 'place of pigs':

> And with his disciples [Dyfrig] stayed [in the place] for many years. They named the place Mochros. *Moch*, that is 'pigs' and *ros*, that is 'place'. *Moch ros* in the British language means 'place of pigs', fittingly place of pigs, since on the preceding night an angel appeared to [Dyfrig] in a dream saying to him, 'The place which you have selected and chosen, in the next day, walk over the whole of it, and where you shall find a white sow lying with her piglets, there found and build your living-place (*habitaculum*) and chapel (*oraculum*) in the name of the Holy Trinity.[23]

The word *ros* can mean 'heath', which well-describes the unclaimed land where swine roam, on which a monk might build a chapel. As we saw in Chapter 3, a white sow showing a monk where to build a monastery is a frequent theme in Anglo-Norman saints' Lives—those of Illtud and of Cyngar, whose monastery was at Congresbury in Somerset, relate a similar story and contain the same themes of a white pig, a dwelling and a chapel, and a dedication to the Holy Trinity.[24]

A Llandaf charter describes a monk named Comereg as abbot of *Mochros* (Moccas); he also may have been a bishop, since a bishop named Comereg features in another Llandaf

St Dyfrig's church, Moccas, Hereford and Worcester.

charter. This suggests that Moccas may have been an early monastic site, and would provide a reason for the *Book of Llandaf's* claim that Bishop Dyfrig was associated with this community.[25]

Moccas church appears to be set within an oval churchyard, typical of an early site, but this is not, in fact, an original feature; while it is likely that there was an early monastery here, the churchyard was laid out by Capability Brown. An eighteenth-century estate map predating Brown's work shows a small rectangular churchyard on the south side of the church only, while a later eighteenth-century plan, made soon after Brown landscaped the park, shows the church surrounded by a ring of trees.[26]

The church at Moccas probably dates from the mid-twelfth century; it has an apse at each end, and no aisles. Formerly, there appears to have been a larger church beside it; in the seventeenth century, Silas Taylor wrote that 'in the churchyard at Moccas are to be seen the foundations of a very large church to which this [one] standing was but a chapple'.[27]

Dyfrig's Burial

According to the *Book of Llandaf*, Dyfrig retired to Bardsey Island in old age and died there. This cannot be verified, but early bishops were, in fact, buried on island retreats, or at least desired this. Six hundred years later, since Llandaf was eager to acquire a patron saint, Dyfrig's body was 'discovered' on Bardsey and translated to Llandaf. His place of burial was (dubiously) identified 'from the monumental tombs of old persons and the writings of very ancient authors'. The Life asserts that Dyfrig had been bishop of Llandaf—a statement found nowhere else, but which was central to Llandaf's claims to property and status among the Welsh dioceses.

Another saint's Life in the *Book of Llandaf* is that of Elgar, a hermit on Bardsey. Its author grandly informs us of the translation of Dyfrig's relics in his final paragraph:

> In the year 1120, on Friday 7 May ... the relics of St Dubricius were translated to Llandaf by Bishop Urban, and with the consent of Ralph [d'Escures], Archbishop of Canterbury, and with the assent of David, Bishop of Bangor, and of Gruffuydd [ap Cynan], king of Gwynedd, and with the approval of the entire clergy and populace, and on Sunday 23 May they were received into the church of Llandaf.[28]

The translation of the bones of Dyfrig from Bardsey to Llandaf, with full pomp and honour, was probably the occasion for the composition of the twelfth-century *Life of Dyfrig*, which also sought to confirm the supremacy in south Wales of the see of Llandaf.[29] Because this was its aim, it contains few historical facts about Dyfrig. Since the much-earlier *Life of Samson* refers to Dyfrig only in passing and at intervals, Dyfrig remains a shadowy, though nevertheless significant, figure in early Welsh Christianity.

Saints of South-East Wales: Paulinus and Cadog

The earliest evidence of Christianity in Wales can be found in the Roman towns of south-east Wales, where excavations have shown that the countryside was well-populated and the people were prosperous and organised. Here, British Christianity survived into post-Roman Wales, though to a limited extent.[1] The two chief Roman towns of Wales were Carmarthen (the capital of the *Demetae*) in the south-west and Caerwent (the tribal capital of the *Silures*) in the south-east. The other major town was Caerleon, 8 miles west of Caerwent, which was the headquarters of the Second Legion Augusta. There were also a number of smaller towns and roadside settlements.

Evidence of Christian worship has been found in Roman Caerwent, and, as we saw in Chapter 1, two soldiers from Caerleon were martyred on account of their faith. Apart from the Welsh Marches and the south coast, Wales was administered through the Roman army, with its network of roads and forts. After Christianity became the official religion of the Roman Empire, soldiers coming from Gaul and other parts of the Roman Empire are likely to have been Christian, but beyond the towns, Christianity may not have spread far in Roman Wales.[2]

Christians in Caerwent

Caerwent was the largest centre of civilian population in Roman Wales. One can still walk round its impressive walls with their defensive towers. There appears to be evidence of a house church; in 1906 a fragmentary pewter bowl was found, with a chi-rho symbol for Christ roughly scratched on its base. It was discovered in house VIIN, opposite the north-east corner of the forum; the graffito was noticed only in 1961. The bowl was found together with seven late fourth-century pottery vessels and a knife in a sealed urn set into the floor, and it has been suggested that the utensils could be part of an *agape* set, designed for use during the meal that followed the Sunday Eucharist.[3]

Nash-Williams identified what he thought was a Christian church in Caerwent, but it was, in fact, a post-medieval cottage. However, two early cemeteries were found—one outside the town and one surrounding the medieval church. After the Romans withdrew, burial continued outside the east gate of the town. Over 118 burials, including some long-cist (or slab-lined) graves, have been found in this partially explored cemetery, which dates from the mid-fourth to the mid-tenth century. It is not known if this became a Christian cemetery.[4]

The second cemetery, inside the town near the present church of St Tathan, was in use from the mid-fourth to the mid-eighth century and is likely to have been used by Christians. The *Life of Tathan* (or 'Tatheus' in Latin), dating from around 1200, claims that an Irish monastery was founded within the town in the fifth or sixth century, but the earliest reference to a monastery at Caerwent dates from the mid-tenth century, when it is mentioned in a Llandaf charter.[5]

An ancient yew tree stands in the churchyard (see photo opposite); it predates the church and indicates an early holy site. Roman masonry is incorporated into the church walls, and a Saxon font has a Roman column for its base. We know little about Tathan. His late—and unhistorical—Life describes him as the 'Father of all Gwent. He was the defender of the woodland country…. He was never angry…. Whatever was given to him, he gave to others … no one was more generous in the West for receiving guests and giving them hospitality.' According to his Life, Tathan was buried beneath the floor of his church (ch. 17). A fragment of a disc-headed cross slab, dating from the tenth or eleventh century, was found in the churchyard, suggesting a continuing monastic presence in Caerwent.

Julius and Aaron

At nearby Caerleon, where the tidal river was still navigable, the Romans built the legionary fortress of Isca; the name Caerleon means 'Camp of the Legions'. Troops could assemble here, their supplies easily transported by land or sea. Writing in the sixth century, Gildas describes two martyred soldiers, Julius and Aaron, who 'displayed the highest spirit in the battle-line of Christ' (*De Excidio* 2. 10); they were arrested at Caerleon and executed for their Christian beliefs.

The church at Caerleon is built over the *principia* (or legionary headquarters), where the imperial standards were kept and statues of the emperor were venerated. It may have been here that Julius and Aaron refused to pay homage to the deified emperor. Beneath the churchyard, the fine mosaic floor of the *principia* was discovered. It depicts a labyrinth; around its border, a stylised tree of life emerges from a vase (see colour plate 4). The mosaic is now preserved in the museum across the road.

Caerleon's medieval church, dedicated to St Cadog, was beside the crossroads at the town centre. Part of a ninth-century high cross survives, decorated with bird-like angels and interlaced patterns; it formerly stood at the crossroads. The Roman ruins in Caerleon provided immense supplies of good building stone, and almost all of the town's older buildings utilise recycled Roman material. Incorporated into the fifteenth-century tower of the church are red sandstone blocks, orange brick tiles, and yellow freestone, all of Roman origin.

Not far from the church are the legionary barracks where Julius and Aaron would have slept, and the giant amphitheatre where the soldiers trained. After their arrest, the two men

Above left: Yew tree in St Tathan's churchyard, Caerwent, Monmouthshire.

Above right: The tidal River Usk at Caerleon, Newport.

would have been sent to the civil settlement of Caerwent, eight miles to the east, to be tried by the judiciary. As Roman citizens, they would not have been subjected to the sadistic indignities of the amphitheatre games at Caerleon; instead, they were probably beheaded, in about AD 304. Ironically, within ten years the converted Emperor Constantine gave Christians freedom to worship.

According to later tradition, Julius and Aaron were buried south-east of the town, across the river, in the Christian portion of a Roman cemetery. It lies in the present parish of Christchurch, on a wooded ridge across the river, at Bulmore on Mount St Albans. Stone-lined burials were found here, and a cross slab dating from the tenth or eleventh century. The presence of a church or chapel on Mount St Albans is first noted in a Llandaf charter that records the donation of the *sanctorum martrium iulij et aaron* ('the shrine of saints Julius and Aaron'); the chapel is referred to in other twelfth- and thirteenth-century sources, and again in the fifteenth century.[6]

Brychan

In early times, Irish families migrated to south Wales in search of land. Brychan, who may have lived in the sixth century, was the legendary dynastic founder of the early medieval kingdom of Brycheiniog (which included the middle Usk valley in south-east Wales), but nothing historically reliable is known about him. The foundation legends of Brycheiniog, or Brecon, are contained in two medieval texts—*De Situ Brecheniauc* ('*About Brycheiniog*') and *Cognacio Brychan* ('*The kin of Brychan*').[7] They were written in or near Brecon in the late tenth or eleventh century, and survive only in later versions.

They describe Teuderic (or Tewdrig) as the king of the district, perhaps in the fifth century. Teuderic claimed descent from a Roman nobleman, and lived at a place called Garth Matrun, which has been equated with Talgarth. Brychan apparently established the kingdom of Brycheiniog by expanding his grandfather's territory, and by the seventh and eighth century Brycheiniog had emerged as one of the British kingdoms in Wales.[8]

The foundation texts describe how Brychan's family landed in south-west Wales and travelled east along ancient routes to the hilly region of Brecon, where they settled. His mother, Marcella (or Marchell in Welsh), returned to Ireland during a severe winter in order to marry an Irish prince. The frost killed many of the warriors who accompanied Marcella, but her father had had a fur coat made for her, and she arrived safely. She gave birth to a son before returning home and named him Broccán, which means 'Little Badger'.

As a youth, Brychan was sent to the kingdom of Powys as a resident hostage; this was an early custom whereby neighbouring kingdoms kept peace with each other. He violated the king's daughter and fathered Cynog, who later became a holy man. He married three times and had twelve sons and twenty-four daughters according to the earliest lists, and more in later ones; different versions include different names.

Churches dedicated to Brychan's children are found in Wales, south-east Ireland, Devon, Cornwall, and Brittany. Some of these may date from early times, but Brychan was popular in late medieval times, and many more churches were then named after his family. Although Brychan may have been a legendary chieftain, a large number of ogham inscriptions are found in Brecon, which suggests Irish settlement, perhaps as early as the fifth century.

Paulinus

We learn about one, or perhaps two, early Welsh saints named Paulinus from a *Life of Paul Aurélien*, which was completed in 884 by Wromonoc, a monk of Landévennec in Brittany; it is preserved in two early manuscripts.[9] It is likely that Wromonoc's Life is concerned with a Breton saint rather than a Welsh one, but since nothing was known about his origins, Wromonoc borrowed information from elsewhere about his supposed early life in Wales. This information provides us with clues about a Paulinus after whom churches and chapels are named around Llandovery in Carmarthenshire.

Wromonoc's *Life of Paul Aurélien* is divided into two books. Book One, which describes Paul's life in south Wales, relates that Paul (surnamed Aurélien, the son of a count named Perphirius) was a native of Penychen, in south-east Glamorgan. Here, Wromonoc appears to identify Paul Aurélien with 'Poul Pennichen', who is mentioned in the *Life of Cadog*. Wromonoc then shifts the location of his story, and probably the identity of its subject, and describes how Paul and his eight brothers lived in a district called Brehant Dincat, which Doble identifies with Llandingat (meaning Llandovery) in Carmarthenshire.[10]

We are told that Paul was placed by his parents in the school of Illtud, where David, Samson, and Gildas were fellow pupils. At the age of sixteen, Paul left Illtud's monastery to live as a hermit at Llanddeusant, in Carmarthenshire, where he was ordained priest by an unnamed bishop. Later, at the request of King Mark (probably a Cornish king), he moved to Cornwall, and he eventually migrated to Brittany with twelve disciples. Book 2 describes Paul's work in Brittany, where his chief foundation was the bishopric of St Pol-de-Léon. He died at an advanced age on the island of Batz.

Although evidence for a Welsh saint named Paulinus is limited, it is likely that he existed; in the parish of Llandingad, churches at Capel Peulin and Nant-bai and a holy well, Ffynnon Beulin, are named after him. At Llangors, in neighbouring Brecon, the church of Llanbeulan is named after Paulinus (or Peulan in Welsh), while Llan y Deuddeg Sant, or 'church of the twelve saints' perhaps echoes the twelve disciples of Paul Aurélien.[11]

Two Early Inscriptions

The remains of a tall, thin pillar stone found at Cynwyl Gaeo, near Llandovery in Carmarthenshire, commemorates a man named Paulinus. Its two-line metrical inscription in debased Roman capitals reads:

SERVATUR FID[A]EI, PATRI[A]EQUE SEMPER AMATOR
HIC PAULINUS IACIT, CULTOR PIENTIS[S]IMUS AEQUI

This can be translated as

Preserver of the Faith, constant lover of his country,
here lies Paulinus, the devoted champion of righteousness.[12]

A second inscription may or may not refer to the same person; it is found on a pillar stone from the parish of Llantrisant (or 'church of three saints') in central Anglesey, 8 miles east of Holyhead; its style of lettering is similar to that of the inscription from Llandovery. This is the longest known memorial inscription from Western Britain dating from the fifth to the early seventh century. Unusually, it commemorates a woman, much of whose name is missing, but most of the inscription is about her husband, who was a priest or possibly a bishop (the Latin word is *sacerdos*) in Anglesey in the sixth century. It demonstrates an organised church in Anglesey at this early time, and also shows that it was not unusual for priests to be married.

Fifteen lines survive from the inscription which, in English, means:

…iva, a most holy woman, lies here, who was the very loving wife of Bivatig[irnus], servant of God, priest and disciple ['vasso'] of Paulinus, by race a […]docian, and an example to all his fellow citizens and relatives both in character, in rule of life, [and] of wisdom, which is better than gold from gems.[13]

The term *vasso*, resembling our word 'vassal', is a Gaulish word meaning 'servant' or 'disciple'; this priest was *vasso Paulini*, a disciple of Paulinus. The inscription is carved in mixed Roman capitals with a few half-uncials, and dates from the mid- or late sixth century. Its language resembles European and African Roman Christian inscriptions of the period. The slab is now in Gwynedd Museum and Art Gallery, in Bangor.

Six miles south of Llantrisant on Anglesey, standing alone in farmland, is the church of Llanbeulan (or '*llan* of Paulinus'). It contains a very fine early eleventh-century font, which may once have been a pre-Norman shrine.[14] The font is likely to have come from the same workshop as one of the great crosses at Penmon Priory (see Chapter 8).[15] The church can be found by driving south on A4080; it is just past Engedi, and is visible in a field, down a short lane.

Paulinus in Rhygyfarch's *Life of David*

Paulinus is mentioned in a number of medieval Lives of other saints. The Life of Teilo in the *Book of Llandaf* names Teilo as one of the disciples of the 'wise man', Paulinus. The *Life of Cybi*, however, describes Paulinus as a disciple of Cybi, although this may refer to a different Paulinus. Rhygyfarch's *Life of David*, written in the late eleventh century, describes how David spent ten years studying under Paulinus, whose name evidently still commanded respect:

> After that, [David] went to the scholar Paulinus, a disciple of the holy bishop Germanus, who … led a life pleasing to God. Saint David remained there many years studying the bible and following what he studied.[16]

Rhygyfarch also hints that David was his equal because, as we saw in Chapter 3, he healed the elderly man of blindness.

The mention of Germanus is anachronistic; it refers to Germanus of Auxerre, who visited Britain in 429 and in around 445, well before David's time, but Rhygyfarch includes him to emphasise the importance of Paulinus. Later in Rhygyfarch's *Life of David*, Paulinus is the elderly bishop who advises that David be invited to the Synod of Brefi. Again, Rhygyfarch depicts Paulinus praising young David as greater than himself:

> And standing up, one of the bishops, called Paulinus, with whom the holy pontiff, David, had once studied, said, 'There is one who was made a bishop by the Patriarch, who has not yet been present at our synod. He is an eloquent man, full of grace, whose religion is proven; he is the companion of angels, an amiable man, good looking, with a splendid figure, and four cubits in height. I therefore advise you to invite him'.[17]

Llangors

Llangors is a small town, 6 miles east of Brecon in south-east Wales, in the foothills of the Black Mountains. The full name of the settlement was Llan yn y Gors, or 'church in the marsh'. It is dedicated to Paulinus and stands on what appears to be an early site, within what was formerly a curvilinear churchyard, beside a stream. It is thought that there was a monastery here from the seventh century until, perhaps, the Norman conquest of Wales. It seems to have no longer existed by 1152, when the Prior of Brecon nominated a priest to serve the church at Llangors.

Two memorial stones now inside the church indicate an early cemetery. A sixth- or seventh-century memorial stone is inscribed +GURCI BLEDRUS, or 'Gurci's cross, [erected by] Bledrus'. A later bilingual stone, decorated with pockmark patterns, perhaps dates from the eleventh or twelfth century.[18] Its inscription, in Latin and ogham, reads 'HIC IACET SIWERD FILIVS VVLMER', or 'Here lies Siwerd, son of Vulmer'. These men have Anglo-Saxon names.

According to a charter in the *Book of Llandaf*, Awst (Welsh for 'Augustus'), King of Brycheiniog, gave the bodies of himself and his sons, Eiludd and Rhiwallon, to the church at *Llan Cors* for burial; this may indicate that Llangors was a royal burial ground. Another charter records that King Awst, who lived in the first half of the eighth century, gave to Bishop Euddogwy and his successors a royal estate (*territorium*), the boundaries of which appear to correspond to the parish of Llangors. The grant also included its fish and its eel fishery as a form of food rent, so the estate must have included Llangors Lake, half a mile south-west of the present settlement. The charters appear to date from the eighth century, but may, in fact, be no earlier than the tenth century.[19]

Llangors Crannog

The kingdom of Brycheiniog was attacked from various quarters, and its ruler sought protection from the Anglo-Saxon King Alfred. In 896, Viking raiders devastated parts of the kingdom; a crannog was built in Llangors Lake, perhaps in response to the raids. Llangors Lake is the largest natural lake in south Wales; the crannog (see colour plate 2) is situated 40 m from its northern shore. It is an artificial island which today measures 40 m across and is covered by trees and reeds. Its construction required an ability to call upon a high level of specialised knowledge and resources. The crannog was formerly occupied by buildings which periodically may have housed the *llys*, or court, of the king of Brycheiniog.

The crannog at Llangors is the only one to have been identified in Wales, although there are many in Scotland and Ireland. The name crannog is derived from the Irish word *crann*, meaning a tree; this refers to the common use of timber in their construction. Crannogs were created by driving piles into the mud; an artificial island was then built up in layers of various available materials until it rose above the surface of the water. Crannogs were principally defensive in purpose. Most show gaps in their palisade, usually facing the shore, where boats could land; some, like that at Llangors, were reached by a causeway. The occupants usually lived by farming around the lake shore and by fishing.

Llangors crannog may not have been in use for more than a century, since Manuscript B of the Anglo-Saxon Chronicle relates that shortly before midsummer in 916, the Saxon King Æthelflæd sent an army to Wales to destroy 'the palace on the lake'; they captured the queen and thirty-three of the king's followers.[20] In the 1190s, in his *Journey Through Wales*, Gerald of Wales recorded a folk memory of the destruction of the island palace of Llangors. Local inhabitants said there was a town beneath the waters of the lake; sometimes the city could be seen floating on its surface. They said that the lake sometimes turned bright green, and occasionally scarlet. These changes of colour were thought to herald an invasion, but are now believed to have been caused by be algae blooms.[21]

In the sixteenth century, the remains of timber planks forming the crannog's palisade could still be seen, floating in the water. The crannog was observed in the late 1860s by two local antiquarians, Edgar and Henry Dumbleton, after the lake level had been lowered. They described a substantial mound of boulders lying on top of brushwood, reeds and sand. They noted that the south and west sides of the mound were still edged by one or two oak palisades.[22]

The crannog was excavated in 1989–90; it was found that the island had been periodically extended from an initial platform. Timber from earlier structures was incorporated into later ones. Dating of one sample gave a tree-ring sequence of AD 747–859, suggesting construction in the ninth and early tenth centuries. In 1925 a log canoe had been found here, dated to around 800; it is now in the museum at Brecon.

During the excavations, part of a handle from a portable, house-shaped reliquary was found; it was decorated with blue glass studs and red and yellow enamel work. It resembles Irish models, and is likely to predate the tenth century, when the site was probably destroyed by Mercian forces. Important individuals, in addition to churches, might possess relics; a letter issued by Dafydd ap Llywelyn in 1241 noted that Dafydd 'has sworn on the holy cross that he has carried around with him'. This may explain why fragments of a reliquary were found in the crannog—it could have housed relics belonging to Tewdwr ap Elised, King of Brycheiniog at the time of the site's destruction.[23] Alternatively, a monk may have visited the island palace, taking the reliquary with him.

During the excavations of the 1880s, bone, charcoal and a few fragments of leather, pottery, and metal were found. The excavations in 1989–90 recovered evidence of animal husbandry and cereal cultivation. Smelting was suggested by fragments of fired clay from furnace linings or hearths, and slag. A bone comb was found, and rare pieces of intricately-patterned cloth. The fine quality of its weave, and indeed the carefully-planned construction of the entire site, indicates that Llangors was the home of one of the leading families of ninth- and tenth-century Wales.[24]

Cadog

Like Paulinus, Cadog was a notable figure among the monks of south-east Wales in the sixth century, but since the two earliest Lives of Cadog were written 500 years after his death, they have little historical value. Cadog is, however, mentioned in earlier Irish texts, in which he is presented as a teacher of Irish monks who sought him out in Britain. The first *Life of Cadog* was written by Lifris of Llancarfan in the late eleventh century, with the purpose of honouring the monastery of Llancarfan and confirming its privileges; it is unique among Welsh Lives in its length and its detail. After the Norman conquest of Glamorgan, Llancarfan was annexed by Gloucester Abbey; the *Life of Cadog* was subsequently reworked for a wider audience by Caradog of Llancarfan in the early twelfth century.

Lifris is concerned to emphasise the authority of Cadog, nicknamed 'the Wise', whose superiority is acknowledged not only in Wales, but even in Rome. Lifris relates that Gildas refused to sell Cadog a 'beautiful mottled bell', and instead took it to Rome as a gift for the pope. But the bell would not ring for him, and the pope commanded Gildas to give it to Cadog, saying: 'For two reasons will all the Britons reverence this bell, because it was owned by me, and because it has been owned by St Cadog' (ch. 27).[25]

Cadog works miracles like those of the great Old Testament figure of Moses. Lifris recounts that Cadog created a spring with a stick while travelling in Cornwall, just as the Book of Numbers in the Old Testament describes Moses striking a rock in the desert to give water to the thirsty Israelites (Numbers 20. 2–11). Cadog's spring brings healing:

> For if any sick person drink from that fount, trusting firmly in the Lord, he shall receive soundness of belly and bowels, and he will throw up in his vomit all slimy worms out of himself [ch. 31].

The manuscript containing Cadog's Life also contains an account of his supposed martyrdom at Benevento, in southern Italy; this may have been a device to explain why Llancarfan did not possess his body. The next text in the manuscript is an account of miracles worked by Cadog in Glamorgan after his death, starting with an account of how Cadog's shrine and other relics were saved from raiding Danes and Englishmen. This is followed by genealogies of Cadog, the story of how his parents entered religious life, and a collection of charters and other accounts of tributes due to the monastery.

The entire collection dates from various periods, and the Life itself sets out in narrative form the status and privileges of Cadog and Llancarfan. At this time, there was considerable rivalry between monasteries; by the twelfth century, there were thirty-six communities in south-east Wales. As we have seen, however, Cadog's monastery of Llancarfan did not survive the Norman advance into south Wales—it was dissolved in around 1086.

Cadog's Supposed Origins

According to Lifris, Cadog was of noble birth. His father, Gwynllyw, to whom Newport Cathedral is dedicated, was a prince of Gwent in south-east Wales, while his mother Gwladys was a daughter of Brychan, the ruler of Brecon, which lay to the north-east of Gwent. Cadog thus belonged to one of the local dynasties of Welsh chieftains who ruled the region when the Romans withdrew in the early fifth century. Both Cadog and Illtud may have worked among the descendants of Romano-British Christians. The *Life of Cadog* comments on his Roman culture; he loves the works of Virgil and regrets that, as a Christian, he would be unable to meet the pagan poet in heaven!

There is a cluster of churches dedicated to Cadog in the upper Usk valley, centred on Llangattock-nigh-Usk (or 'church of Cadog near the Usk') in his father's territory, 5 miles north-west of Abergavenny. Lifris relates that Cadog had been baptised in the nearby Onneu Brook, and later returned to evangelise the people in the hill-fort across the river. The broad River Usk has carved a valley at the foot of the hill-fort; the name 'Usk' comes from a Celtic word meaning 'water'. Today sheep graze in Llangattock churchyard, around the squat twelfth-century tower and the Tudor porch. Inside, the church is spacious; a fourteenth-century arcade divides the double chancel and nave.

Cadog Establishes Llancarfan

Lifris recounts that as a youth, Cadog studied at Caerwent, in Tathan's monastery. He later founded a community of his own at Llancarfan, 4 miles north-west of Barry, and a group of monks from Caerwent joined him. Lifris describes Paulinus as his uncle, making him King Pawl of Penychen. Pawl owns, and gives to his nephew, the valley in which Cadog builds the monastery of Llancarfan. Its name means 'church of the stags', which Lifris explains as follows: when Cadog asked two monks to till the ground near the monastery, they refused, but a pair of stags appeared from the woods and dug the soil with their antlers.

When a monk founded a monastery, it was important that he should discover the place where God wanted him to live. Before selecting his site at Llancarfan, Cadog and his monks spent the night in prayer, and in the morning a white boar appeared to indicate where he should begin building. As we have seen, this is a recurring theme in stories of Celtic saints' foundations—the white boar becomes a messenger from God. In Chapters 3 and 4 we saw how a wild white boar showed both Brynach and Dyfrig where to build their chief monastery.

The earliest of these pig foundation tales is found in the *Life of Cadog* by Lifris. Cadog prays for a sign from God to know where to build a church on the land which he has been given, partly through the agency of a swineherd. An angel appears and tells him that he will find a place on which to build an *oratorium*, and that he will see an old bristly white boar leap out and land in three separate places to indicate where he should build a *templum* in the name of the Holy Trinity, a dormitory and refectory.[26] The similarities between this foundation story and those in the twelfth-century Lives of Dyfrig and Illtud show how monastic biographers copied one another.

In his *Life of Cadog*, Lifris relates that each monk owned a dwelling, with a portion of land and servants to till it, and each one cared for orphans and guests; this sounds rather different from a monastery as we know it. Lifris describes the abbot's dwelling (*habitaculum*) and those of the teacher (*doctor*) and priest (*sacerdos*). It has been suggested that this was perhaps a hazy monastic memory of former times, an attempt to recall a

St Cadog's church, Llangattock-nigh-Usk, Powys.

The River Usk below Llangattock-nigh-Usk, Powys.

well-organised post-Roman mother church, whose teacher was Cadog, as was Lifris in his own day.[27]

There were several great monasteries in the Vale of Glamorgan—that of Illtud at Llanilltud Fawr, only 5 miles west of Llancarfan, and that of Docco at Llandough, now a northern suburb of Penarth, further to the east. Llancarfan was beside a stream not far from the sea, which has now receded. It may have been an ancient port, safely upstream, hidden from pirates. Like Llanilltud Fawr, it was near the main road through south Wales, and far enough up the Bristol Channel to provide an easy sea-crossing to south-west Britain, and so to mainland Europe.

The Celtic monastery at Llancarfan probably lies below the field to the south of the present church; a well in the next field is also associated with the monastery. It became a centre of learning, with a large number of monks. The twelfth-century *Chronicle of the Princes* records the destruction of Llancarfan by Vikings in 988. As the centre of Cadog's cult, Llancarfan once housed a shrine containing his relics, which was moved elsewhere for safekeeping in the face of enemy attack; The *Life of Cadog* relates that during the conflict, a Viking broke a 'gilded wing' from the reliquary, which seems to have been lost by the twelfth century.[28]

According to Lifris, Cadog was martyred; while the elderly abbot was celebrating the Eucharist in his monastery at Llancarfan, a Saxon warrior entered the church on horseback and pierced him with a lance. The present church is medieval; its fine, carved-oak screen dates from the Perpendicular period. In recent times, medieval wall paintings have been discovered beneath its white wall plaster.

Carved oak screen, St Cadog's church, Llancarfan, Glamorgan.

The Cult of Cadog Elsewhere

The island of Flat Holm, in the Bristol Channel, provided an island retreat for the larger monastic site on the mainland at Llancarfan. Part of a recumbent slab with a cross was found on the island. Lifris names this and other sites, including Barry Island and Llanmaes, closer to Llanilltud Fawr, as dependant or daughter churches of Llancarfan. Cadog's cult spread both north and south. A chapel and holy well were named after him at Cadoc Farm in Harlyn Bay, on the north Cornish coast, and an early church is dedicated to Cadog at Quethiock, 4 miles east of Liskeard; there are also several Scottish sites where Cadog is honoured.

In Brittany there are fourteen dedications to Cadog, but the Breton Cadog may have been another saint. Lifris relates that, after establishing the monastery of Llancarfan, he crossed the English Channel and landed on the Île de Cado, a small island in the mouth of the River Etel in southern Brittany. Lifris writes that Cadog spent three years here, and founded a priory on the island that is now linked to the mainland by a causeway.[29]

Cadog's holy well on the seashore can be seen in colour plate 5: to the left is the roof of the well house, and its back wall is built into the rock face. To the right is the well pool, in which pilgrims could bathe. It contains fresh water, except when it is covered at high tide. Beyond the well house, a chapel contains an ancient slab known as St Cado's bed; a saint's 'bed' was often his tomb. Cado's bed contains a hollow, into which the deaf place their heads in the hope of healing. The chapel became a centre for pilgrimage, especially for the deaf.

Llancarfan's Charters

The fifteen chapters which follow the account of Cadog's life are a list of charters that describe the donation of land to the church at Llancarfan. In some of the charters, a donor makes a grant 'for his soul' (*pro anima N*), so that his name might be written in the *Book of Cadog*: this ensured that the community would pray for him. The book is now lost; it appears to have been a gospel book, whose authorship was attributed to Gildas.[30]

From the eighth century, as kinship groups gave land to churches, the clear definition of boundaries became increasingly important; these were not only recorded in charters, but also marked out on the ground. The *Life of Cadog* records how the monastery exchanged a piece of land for a township named Conguoret, which was owned by two men named Spois and Rodri. Rodri was given a charter that spelt out the transaction, and then:

> afterwards Rodri and Spois and his sons came together, Conigre [the abbot] also, and his clergy brought the cross of Saint Cadog and his earth, and going round the aforesaid land of Conguoret, claimed it, and scattered the earth of the aforesaid saint upon it in the presence of suitable witnesses in token of permanent possession (ch. 55).[31]

In this way the exchange was celebrated by a liturgical act, witnessed by both God and the people, with Cadog represented by the earth on which he trod.

St Canna of Llangan

Canna is another Glamorgan saint; she is one of the few female saints commemorated in south Wales, both at Llangan near Whitland, in Carmarthenshire, and at Llangan, 12 miles west of Cardiff, in the Vale of Glamorgan. She was a Breton princess who came to Wales with her husband Sadwrn and their son Crallo, according to the unreliable writings of Iolo Morganwg—this being the bardic name of Edward Williams (1747–1826).

At Llangan in Glamorgan, aerial photography has revealed a circular churchyard within a larger circular enclosure, just north of the present church. Near the porch is the upper portion of a disc-headed cross slab, 1 m wide and 1.3 mm high, carved from sandstone. It dates from the late ninth or the tenth century, and depicts the crucifixion. Until the twelfth century, Christ on the cross was portrayed in carvings as living, rather than dead. On the cross at Llangan, Christ is depicted alive, with open eyes and extended arms. He appears to be bearded, and wears a loincloth; he is flanked by the smaller figures of soldiers with a sponge (left) and a spear (right).[32]

The style of carving is reminiscent of similar scenes found on Irish metalwork; there is only one similar cross in Wales. On the reverse side is a plain Greek cross. The fine quality of the sculpture indicates that this was a site of some status; it is not known whether this was a monastic church or whether the cross was erected by a secular lord.

Cross head depicting the crucifixion, St Canna's church, Llangan, Glamorgan.

There are fragments of another Celtic cross in the church porch, and a plain medieval tub font inside the church. In the graveyard is a fine preaching cross, carved in the fourteenth or fifteenth century. Nearby, Ffynnon Canna was visited as a healing well by pilgrims for many centuries.

Llangan in Carmarthenshire is on the boundary with Pembrokeshire at an ancient strategic site, where the old road from Carmarthen to Haverford West crosses the River Tâf. Here, a holy well is named after Canna, and a boulder is named Canna's Chair. People were cured of the ague and of intestinal complaints by throwing pins into the well, bathing, and then sitting in the chair, a process which was sometimes repeated for fourteen days in order to effect a cure. In about 1840 the watercourse was damaged, and the well is now dry. In 1872, a man aged seventy-eight remembered people undergoing treatment, and said he had seen hundreds of pins thrown into the well as offerings.[33]

Llangan near Whitland is thought to have been the site of an occasional residence of King Hywel Dda, or Hywel 'the Good' (*c.* 880–950), who is termed King of the Britons in the *Annales Cambriae* and the *Annals of Ulster*. He made submission to King Athelstan of England, in an agreement whereby both men jointly ruled parts of Wales. Hywel Dda is said to have summoned to Llangan representatives from the regions he ruled, in order to codify Welsh law; parts of this legal system remained in use until the sixteenth century.

Tewdrig of Mathern

At the extreme eastern end of south Wales, beside the M48, near the Welsh end of the Severn Bridge, is the village of Mathern, a mile south of Chepstow. In earlier times, this was marshland, where the River Wye flowed into the Severn. The river reached Mathern; a former harbour is now covered by low-lying fields. The area was ruled by the family of Tewdrig, and Mathern's former name was Merthyr Tewdrig; the later name Ma Teyrn, or 'the place of a king', is first found in the thirteenth century.

According to the twelfth-century *Book of Llandaf*, Tewdrig was a seventh-century king of Gwent and Glywysing. He transferred the crown to his son, Meurig ap Tewdrig, before becoming a hermit at Tintern. He was recalled to fight the Saxons from over the River Wye, and won, but was mortally wounded. His body was brought to Mathern to be taken to the island of Flat Holm in the Bristol Channel, where he had asked to be buried, but he died at Mathern.

The *Book of Llandaf* relates that Meurig gave the church and its surrounding land, extending for several miles, to the bishops of Llandaf. Tewdrig was said to have been buried beneath the chancel of the church. The supposed bones of Tewdrig were unearthed in the seventeenth century, but they would have been those of a later medieval dignitary since they were found in a stone coffin, which is not a feature of early medieval burials.[34] The present church is Norman and Early English. Beside the lane that leads to the church is Tewdrig's well, in a square pool. According to legend, this is where his wounds were washed after his fatal battle.

The former name of the village, Merthyr Tewdrig, may date from early times. The word

St Tewdrig's
well, Mathern,
Monmouthshire.

merthyr derives from the Latin word *martyrium*, meaning a martyr's grave or shrine. Often, *merthyr* is followed by a personal name, when it might indicate a place which possessed the remains of a saint or martyr, such as Merthyr Tydfil. Many such saints, including Cynog, Dyfan and Tydfil, are connected with tales of martyrdom, but it is likely that in time *merthyr* lost its specialised meaning, and later simply meant 'church', because the name-element *merthyr* was sometimes replaced by *llan* (church), *eglwys* (church) or *capel* (chapel).

Nevertheless, there are a number of early sites with the name *merthyr*. Llangaffo on Anglesey was originally Merthyr Caffo; a number of early gravestones have been found around the church. Llanfeirian, a chapel in the parish of Llangadwaladr, also on Anglesey, was originally Merthyr Meirion. Both sites may be named after early saints.[35] Thus Mathern, where the martyred Tewdrig was said to be buried, might be an early *merthyr* site. However, since there have been no early finds at Mathern, its origins remain uncertain.

PART II
SAINTS OF NORTH WALES

The Mid-Wales Coast and Uplands:
Cadfan, Tysilio and Melangell

There are no early Lives of northern saints comparable with the eighth-century *Life of Samson*, who lived in the south. However, there are a considerable number of early inscribed monuments in north Wales that provide clues concerning early Christianity, while poems by court poets tell us how monks such as Cadfan and Tysilio were viewed in later centuries.

Anglesey was the seat of the early kings of Gwynedd, the kingdom which covered much of north Wales, and these chieftains feature in a number of saints' Lives. In later medieval times, Bardsey Island became a focus for pilgrimage, so many saints came to be associated with the island. A few saints lived in the central uplands and on the coast of mid-Wales: sites associated with them will be explored in this chapter.

Cadfan of Tywyn

The twelfth-century *Book of Llandaf* describes a Breton monk named Cadfan who sailed to mid-Wales in the sixth century with twelve followers, and settled beside a spring on the sea shore at Tywyn, halfway between Barmouth and Aberystwyth. Here, Cadfan founded a monastery and was joined by many brothers. This became the chief monastery of Merioneth, and the centre of Cadfan's cult. A poem of praise entitled '*Canu Cadfan*' (or 'Ode to Cadfan'), written by Llewelyn Fardd in the mid-twelfth century, records a number of relics associated with Cadfan, including an altar, a gospel book, and also his crosier.[1] These may have been housed in a small chapel—Capel Cadfan, which stood in the north-west corner of the churchyard until 1620; it perhaps contained his shrine.

Inside the church, a grave-marker dating from around the ninth century commemorates some people from leading families; its worn inscription shows that the wealthy now spoke Welsh. This is one of the earliest examples of written Welsh; until this point, inscriptions were normally in Latin. The inscribed panels are set low down on the shaft, perhaps to be read while kneeling. Also preserved in the church is a semi-circular sundial, dating from early times, carved at the top of a monolith.

By the mid-tenth century, St Cadfan's had become the mother church of the area, although it was destroyed by Vikings in 963. The present church dates from the late eleventh and early twelfth centuries. Cadfan's holy well was north-west of the church, and

St Cadfan's church, Tywyn, Gwynedd.

is now in the grounds of the NatWest bank. The spring was visited for healing until long after the Reformation. Baths and changing rooms were built alongside it; they were pulled down in 1894, by which time they had fallen into disuse.[2]

The Ode to Cadfan speaks of three altars at Tywyn—to Our Lady, St Peter, and, presumably, to Cadfan:

> Mary's altar from the Lord, trustworthy and sacred relic;
> the altar of Peter in his authority which should be praised;
> and the third altar which was bestowed by heaven:
> the dwelling place is blessed because of its hospitality.[3]

It is unclear whether the poem refers to three altars within a single church or three churches, including Capel Cadfan.

The Ode to Cadfan

Canu Cadfan is one of three poems composed around the same time, in praise of Cadfan, Tysilio, and David. They are lengthy, intricate eulogies written by professional court poets, designed to impress a high-status gathering. All three are highly ornate, with elaborate invocations and closing prayers; they are the product of many hours of labour by master craftsmen. The Ode to Cadfan appears to have been commissioned for a specific occasion, and has a political agenda. The poem deliberately alternates between events in the sixth and twelfth centuries; it exalts Cadfan's powers while at the same time focussing on the twelfth-century church of Tywyn and the kingdom of Meirionydd, of which it is the mother church.[4]

Cadfan is described as being of mighty strength in battle and a protector of soldiers; this is a play on the name-element *Cad*, which means 'battle' or 'army'. The poem relates that Cadfan came from Brittany to found a church at Tywyn, although there is little evidence of Cadfan's cult in Brittany. His name is coupled with that of Lleuddad as one of the founding saints of the monastery on Bardsey Island. The poet gives the Ode a political slant by using praise to promote his patrons, both secular and religious; the poem also reinforces Tywyn's traditional legal rights as a sanctuary church. Cadfan is praised for his protective powers, and Tywyn is a place of peace and safety,

> where violent intent does not dare go,
> where no man dares take the needy from the church—
> by the shore of the blue sea, on account of its legal right,
> where no oppression is dared, on account of its right to tribute,
> where I will dare wander about [all my] life.[5]

The poem may have been first performed in the presence of the territorial lord and his followers, as well as the monastic community, at a sensitive time in their relationship. In 1147, Abbot Morfran, who was also steward of Lord Cadwaladr's nearby stronghold of Castell Cynfael, refused to surrender to Cadwaladr's nephews when they attacked the castle and deposed their uncle. The abbot and community of Tywyn were now in a vulnerable position, and diplomacy was required. The court poet of Gwynedd was perhaps commissioned to compose a poem in praise of Cadfan, his church at Tywyn, and his land of Meirionnydd, to be sung in the presence of the new lord, Cynan.[6]

The poet presents an ideal picture of peaceful coexistence in Meirionnydd, the land of Cadfan. References to the lord of the land could apply equally to Cadfan and to Cynan, while Abbot Morfran is likened to St Lleuddad, Cadfan's supposed successor on Bardsey Island. By appearing to acclaim Cadfan and Lleuddad, the poet can in fact praise both Lord Cynan and Abbot Morfran without causing offence to either, and can highlight the need for cooperation between them. As the poet hints, Cynan and Morfran may have been cousins, but when he simultaneously portrays Cadfan and Lleudadd as cousins, he may be re-writing history, for this is not confirmed elsewhere.[7]

> I praise two men as the Lord permits me,
> two fair [men], two blessed [men], two generous givers,
> two wise [men] in authority, in harmony,
> two beloved [men], two fellow-countrymen, two holy men,
> two who perform miracles in order to [spread] light before them,
> two whose gifts, to the satisfaction of suppliants, are unhindered,
> they were two cousins who did not plot treachery:
> [may] Cadfan protect [the] church, [both] he and Lleuddad![8]

The Role of the Poet

The twelfth-century 'Poets of the Princes' (or *Gogynfeirdd*) inherited the bardic task of singing the praises of a king or ruler. Poems such as the Ode to Cadfan were treated with great respect, and a poet's creativity was highly honoured. It was believed that God gave the poet grace to speak on behalf of the Christian community; his tasks were to instruct the people, to address God on their behalf, and to embody God's inspirational power in an almost priestly way.

Bardic grammars and Welsh laws describe how the 'chief poet' won his position through competition, and enjoyed the highest status and the greatest privileges. He was required to compose poems in praise of God and the king, and only he could teach lesser poets. Beneath him was the 'poet of the king's retinue', whose task was to inspire the king's warriors before battle.[9] Cynddelw, the author of the Ode to Tysilio described later in this chapter, observes how a poet's praise contributes to a king's identity when he declaims to the Lord Rhys, 'You without me have no voice; I without you have nothing to say.'[10]

St Trillo

Lesser saints were described as disciples of greater saints, and since Cadfan's monastery at Tywyn was a prominent one, a number of early monks are described as Cadfan's followers. One of these was Trillo, to whom the parish church of Llandrillo-yn-Rhos, a mile north-west of Colwyn Bay, is dedicated. Inside its large churchyard are signs of a smaller, roughly oval enclosure, with the present church near its eastern corner. In the last year of his life, Gruffudd ap Cynan (*c.* 1055–1137), King of Gwynedd, bequeathed ten shillings to the church. Until 1540 the site was known as Dinerth, or 'Fort of the Bear', taking its name from the hill fort above the settlement.

This was probably the cult centre of Trillo, and became the mother church of the area. Although it is difficult to imagine today, the church was on a hill top with what appears to have been a harbour at its base; there is a description of ships 'lying under Llandrillo church'. The present low-lying golf course formed the estuary of the River Ganol.[11]

Half a mile away, a tiny medieval chapel dedicated to Trillo was built on a small island, separated from the mainland by a marshy channel. By 1230, Cistercian monks caught fish in the nearby weir; evidence of medieval fish traps survives. Today, St Trillo's chapel is situated below the Victorian promenade, beside the sea shore (see colour plate 7). Inside the chapel, in front of the altar, is a rectangular pool. This encloses the freshwater spring that Trillo or his unknown follower used for drinking and for baptising converts. Beside the chapel are the foundations of his circular hut.

Thirty miles to the south, 5 miles south-west of Corwen, is another settlement named Llandrillo. Its church was built beside an ancient yew tree, and on the opposite bank of the river that runs through the village is Trillo's well, at the foot of a large oak. Two stories about the well illustrate how, until the fairly recent past, saints were believed to punish those who did not treat their wells with reverence. The spring was originally in the corner

Above left: St Trillo's chapel, Llandrillo-yn-Rhos, Conwy.

Above right: St Trillo's well, Llandrillo, Conwy.

of a low-lying field, but in about 1855 the tenant farmer objected to 'trespassers' visiting the well. It therefore ran dry, and reappeared in a neighbouring farmer's field! In another story, the well dried up because someone threw a dead cat or dog into it. By 1913, the spring no longer flowed except in winter or after heavy rain.[12]

Mael and Sulien

The ancient church of Corwen in mid-Wales is dedicated to Mael and Sulien, who were also said to be followers of Cadfan. Corwen is at the foot of the Berwyn Mountains, beside the fast-flowing River Dee, and the town grew alongside an important route for travellers through the centuries. This was the Roman road along which Welsh drovers also herded their cattle; it later became the A5, the main road from London to Holyhead. Early sculpture, including a free-standing cross, suggests that there was a monastery here; it became the mother church of the area.

The name Corwen means 'stone church' (or, literally, 'choir-white'). This is a Welsh version of the English name Whitchurch, and denotes an important stone church at a time when others were more simply constructed of timber. It was not until the eleventh or twelfth century that stone churches began to replace wooden ones in Wales, a transition which occurred later in Wales than in other parts of Britain. They became common only in the twelfth century, particularly in parts of Wales settled by the Normans.[13]

The church was built at an ancient holy site beside a prehistoric standing stone, named 'The pointed stone in the icy corner' in Welsh. When the building was enlarged in medieval times, the ancient stone was incorporated into the wall of the porch.[14] In the churchyard is a large Bronze Age boulder with seven cup-marks; these might be holes into which libations could be poured. The boulder was 'christianised' some time between the ninth and the twelfth centuries, and used as the base for a tall cross (see photo opposite).

Another church is named after Mael and Sulien in the village of Cwm, on the slopes of the Clwyd range, 5 miles from the Flintshire coast. An earlier church, known as *yr hen Eglwys*, or 'the old church', is said to have been situated higher up the hill. In the late seventeenth century, the antiquarian Edward Lhuyd described three bells which were found on the hillside above the present church. They were named the Yellow, White and Grey Bells, apparently since they were made from different metals.[15] A holy well in the vicarage garden was visited by those with eye diseases; its stone trough is set into the front wall of the vicarage garden, beside the road.[16]

'The pointed stone in the icy corner', Corwen church, Denbighshire.

Pre-Christian boulder with cup marks,
surmounted by a cross, at Corwen,
Denbighshire.

Church of Ss Mael and Sulien, Cwm, Denbighshire.

Tysilio of Meifod

Tysilio was patron of the monastery church at Meifod, in the valley of the River Vyrnwy, 6 miles north-west of Welshpool. Although Tysilio was the chief saint of Powys, the kingdom of north-east Wales, little material relating to him survives apart from a twelfth-century poem composed in his honour, *Canu Tysilio*. Other traditions may be preserved in a fifteenth-century Latin *Life of Suliac*, the patron of Saint Suliac in eastern Brittany. Its author may have borrowed details from a lost Life of Tysilio in order to fill out the story of the Breton saint. In the Latin Life, personal names such as Suliau and place names such as Meibot (Meifod) are written in twelfth-century Welsh, which suggests that manuscripts of a Welsh Life of Tysilio were then circulating in Brittany.

Welsh genealogies claim that Tysilio (whose name means 'My [little] Suliau') belonged to the ruling dynasty of Powys. According to the Breton Life, Tysilio fled from his family home to the monastery at Meifod, where he studied under Abbot Gwyddfarch. He later moved westwards and founded a church on Llandysilio Island, in the Menai Strait, where he lived for seven years before returning to Meifod and succeeding Gwyddfarch as abbot. He then migrated to Brittany.

Meifod

The monastery at Meifod may have had links with the early princes of Powys, but this is documented only in the twelfth century. Today's churchyard of 9 acres may indicate the extent of the monastery, which contained two churches and a chapel. The twelfth-century *Chronicle of the Princes* states that the church of St Mary at Meifod was consecrated in 1156, while in 1160 it records that Madog ap Maredudd was buried at Meifod in the church of St Tysilio; this implies that both churches were in use at that time. A chapel dedicated to Gwyddfarch also stood to the south-east of the main church, in an area no longer in the modern churchyard, but still known as Gwyddfarch's Cemetery (*Mynwent Gwyddfarch*); its remains were visible in the seventeenth century.[17]

The monastery became the mother church of Powys, and perhaps the burial place of its kings. Deep beneath the chancel of the church, a vaulted grave was discovered with a fine, carved coffin slab that might mark a royal burial. It represents the triumph of God over evil, and is bordered by serpents and asymmetrical interlacing patterns. In the centre is a Latin cross, and above it a Greek crucifix, on which hangs Jesus with pierced hands. Its design is unique; it has been variously dated to the ninth–tenth century or the twelfth century.

In his Ode to Tysilio, Cynddelw describes him building a church at Meifod:

> He raised a church with fostering hand;
> a church with bright lights,
> and a chancel for offerings,
> a church above the stream, by the glassy waters,
> a church of Powys, paradise most fair.[18]

Carved cross, St Tyslio's church, Meifod, Powys.

The present Norman church was built in 1154 by Madog ap Maredudd, Prince of Powys, the last ruler under whom Powys experienced political unity and independence. The western end of a twelfth-century aisled church survives in the present nave. Its solid arches are constructed of red sandstone, which was little-used in the area and probably expensive and difficult to obtain. The rest of the church dates from the fourteenth and fifteenth centuries.

It is likely that pilgrims came to venerate Tysilio's relics, including a crosier decorated with golden rivets, described in *Canu Tysilio* (ll. 65). A stone carved with a series of small crosses, probably by pilgrims, is built into a window on the south wall of the south aisle. Gwyddfarch was said to buried outside the monastery on 'Anchorite's Hill' (*Gallt yr Ancr*), although a mound known as 'Gwyddfarch's Bed' (*Gwely Gwyddfarch*) is, in fact, a post-medieval rabbit warren which must have received its name in the seventeenth century or later.[19]

The Ode to Tysilio

The praise poem *Canu Tysilio*, composed by Cynddelw Brydydd Mawr, is our chief surviving Welsh source of information about Tysilio, but the poet's style is cryptic and contains few facts. Tysilio is presented as a priest of the people of Powys and Gwynedd, and is also associated with Anglesey. He is referred to as a grandson of King Cyngen. Details of his lineage agree with that found in Welsh genealogies, where he is described as the son of a king of Powys, an ancestor of its twelfth-century rulers. These were the patrons of Cynddelw, who sang the poem.[20]

The Ode to Tysilio includes two features not found in the Breton Life—Tysilio's early career as a warrior, which emphasised his connection with the princes of Powys, and his death in Wales, which strengthened his position as a religious leader of the Welsh. He is depicted as the principal saint of Powys, and defender of its people against the Northumbrians at the Battle of Maserfelth—which took place in 642, perhaps near Oswestry in mid-Wales. Although its main protagonists were Penda of Mercia and Oswald of Northumbria, according to Welsh tradition an army from Powys also took part. In the Ode to Tysilio, the saint protects the men of Powys.

The poet portrays Tysilio's churches and, simultaneously, the influence of the princes of Powys, as spreading into Gwynedd in the west and Buellt in the south. The churches which Tysilio is said to have built are listed:

> A church of lanterns, a place for Mass,
> a church beyond the green mantle of the sea,
> a church beyond the tide, beyond the court of Dinorben,
> a church of Llydaw, the desire of many,
> the church of Pengwern, the chief sod of the earth,
> the church of Powys, a holy, pure paradise,
> the church of Camarch, a rule of honour for its owner.[21]

The Ode to Tysilio also hints that the future of Powys is under threat; it ends with a plea for God's support, just as Tysilio had supported the people of Powys in the past. The poem appears to be a response to a political crisis; it is an appeal by Meifod's community to Owain Gwynedd to intervene in southern Powys and resolve a power struggle between two cousins, Owain Fychan and Owain Cyfeiliog, both of whom claimed the territory. Owain Cyfeiliog was supported by the English, and won. He also became patron of the Cistercian abbey of Strata Marcella, founded in 1170, and was buried there rather than at Meifod. His predecessor, Madog ap Maredudd (d. 1160) was the last of the princes of Powys to be buried in Tysilio's church at Meifod.[22]

Dedications to Tysilio

Although a number of churches in Powys are dedicated to Tysilio, they are unlikely to have been founded by him since he became associated with Powys at a later date. His cult was fostered by its royal house, which developed his cult centre at Meifod and endowed sites dedicated to Tysilio. His influence also extends to the landscape—Llantysilio Mountain rises to the north-west of Llangollen. The River Dee flows at its foot, and a church dedicated to Tysilio is built on the valley slope, above the river.

On the opposite side of Llantysilio Mountain is another settlement whose church is dedicated to Tysilio, named Bryneglwys, or 'hill church'. The village lies close to the stream in the foreground of the photograph opposite, and the church is just visible within its hilltop enclosure, on a low shoulder of Llantysilio Mountain. The stream is a tributary of the Dee, which acted as a highway for travel through north Wales. Some of the boulders from the first stone church at Bryneglwys can be seen in the west wall of the present church, which was built in around 1570.

1. A pre-Christian standing stone at St Non's Bay, Pembrokeshire.

2. Crannog, Llangors Lake, Powys.

3. St David's church, Caldey Island, Pembrokeshire.

4. Roman labyrinth mosaic, Caerleon. (*Reproduced by kind permission of the National Museum of Wales*)

5. St Cadog's Well, Île de Cado, Lorient, Brittany.

6. St Gwynda's Well, Llanwnda, Pembrokeshire.

7. The chapel on the shore at Llandrillo-yn-Rhos, Conwy.

8. Llandysilio Island, Anglesey.

9. Yew tree in Gwyddelwern churchyard, Denbighshire.

10. Medieval bridge at Aberffraw, Anglesey.

11. St Beuno's church, Pistyll, Gwynedd.

12. The Isle of Llangwyfan, Anglesey.

13. Dyserth waterfall, Denbighshire.

14. Bodfari church, built into the hillside, Denbighshire.

15. Henllan church tower, Denbighshire.

16. St Winifred's well, Woolston, Shropshire.

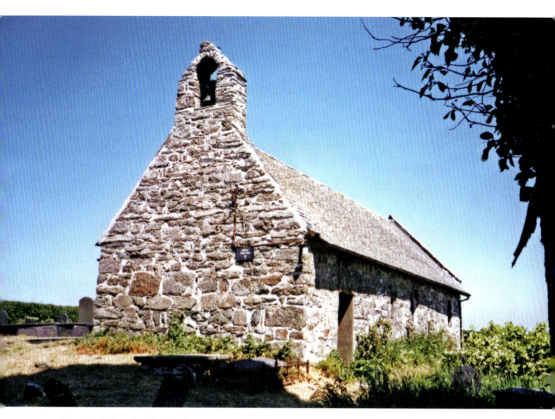

17. Llanbabo church, Anglesey.

18. The River Dee at Bangor Is-coed, Wrexham.

19. Llanfair Pwyllgwyngyll church, Anglesey.

20. St Patrick's chapel, Peel, Isle of Man.

21. Aberdaron church, Gwynedd.

22. Bardsey Island, viewed from the Llŷn peninsula.

23. The ruined Augustinian priory on Bardsey Island.

24. Mynydd Enlli with hut circle in the foreground, Bardsey Island.

Llantysilio Mountain, Denbighshire.

St Tysilio's church, Bryneglwys, Denbighshire, viewed from the village.

Llandysilio Island

Tysilio's Breton Life describes him spending seven years on Llandysilio Island, which can be visited by walking down through the woods, a little beyond the Anglesey end of the Menai Bridge. A single-chambered church, perhaps dating from the fifteenth century, may stand on the site of an earlier chapel (see colour plate 8). The islet is reached by a causeway, from which one can watch curlews, oystercatchers, and a colony of terns. In spring, the island is golden with primroses.

Beyond the church are the Swellies, dangerous tidal currents. An eighteenth-century traveller, Thomas Pennard, described how 'as a very young man, I ventured myself in a small boat into the midst of the boiling waves and mill-race current'.[23] In spite of continuous traffic over the Menai Bridge, Llandysilio Island has retained its peaceful atmosphere through the centuries.

The Life of Melangell

While we possess numerous Lives of Welsh male saints, only three Lives of women survive: the Breton Life of Non (see Chapter 2), a Life of Winifred (see Chapter 7), and that of Melangell (or Monacella, in Latin). Her short Latin Life, *Historia Divae Monacellae*, is found in two versions dating from the late fifteenth or early sixteenth century, although they are probably based on earlier sources. Unlike Non and Winifred, Melangell's cult is confined to a single site—Pennant Melangell, at the head of the remote Tanat valley, in the Berwyn Mountains of mid-Wales. It is situated 20 miles west of Oswestry and 2 miles west of Llangynog.

According to her Life, Melangell was an Irish chieftain's daughter who fled to Wales to escape an arranged marriage, and became a hermit at Pennant Melangell. A local chieftain named Brochwel, King of Powys, who lived in Shrewsbury, was hare-coursing at Pennant Melangell. His hounds raised a hare that fled to a thicket where Melangell was praying. The hare jumped into the folds of her cloak, while the hounds ran away:

> Then the prince cried 'Get it, hounds, get it!' but the more he shouted, urging them on, the further the dogs retreated and, howling, fled from the little animal. Finally, the prince, altogether astonished, asked the girl how long she had lived on her own on his lands, in such a lonely spot. In reply the girl said that she had not seen a human face for these fifteen years.[24]

Brochwel was so impressed that he gave Melangell the valley, where she founded a convent of nuns. In late medieval language, the Life describes how her church was granted the privilege of sanctuary for criminals fleeing from the law. The Life hints that there was a double community of monks and nuns at the site, with its mention of abbots. Brochwel declares:

O most worthy virgin Melangell … I give and present to you most willingly these my lands for the service of God, that they may be a perpetual asylum, refuge and defence, in honour of your name, excellent girl.… But on the other hand, if any wrongdoer who enjoys the protection of your sanctuary shall set out in any direction to do harm, then the independent abbots of your sanctuary, who alone know of their crimes, shall, if they find them in that place, ensure that the culprits be released and handed over to the Powys authorities in order to be punished.[25]

Melangell's Church

The church at Pennant Melangell appears to have been built around her grave. The large oval churchyard had been a pre-Christian holy place; ancient yew trees grow round the enclosure, and excavation has shown that the church is built over a Middle Bronze Age cremation cemetery, dating from about 1200 BC. It is not known whether the church was the focus of a settlement, or if it was isolated in the landscape.[26]

A convent was possibly founded here in the late eighth century. Excavations in 1989 at the western end of the church revealed graves, some beneath the foundations of the twelfth-century building. Large numbers of quartz pebbles had been placed over some of the graves—this was an early custom whereby visitors left behind a token of their prayer.[27]

Unusually, the church had an eastern apse that was entered through an off-centre archway. On the south side of the apse, a grave covered by a large slab and edged with stones has been excavated, and a second slab-covered grave was found beneath the apse wall. In 1959 the grave edged with stones was interpreted as Melangell's grave; this cannot be proven, but the opening into the apse appears to respect the grave.[28] The apse was re-ordered many times: excavation revealed six or seven medieval layers of construction in this small area.[29]

The Romanesque Shrine

The impressive Romanesque shrine of Melangell was reconstructed in the 1950s from many fragments incorporated into the fabric of the church and lychgate. In the twelfth century, with the increasing influence of the Normans in Wales, holy men and women were sometimes moved from their original grave and placed in a new, often raised, tomb or shrine. The Normans built similar shrines in France, and there were a number of elaborate Romanesque shrines in Powys, of which this is the finest.[30]

The house-shaped shrine is behind the main altar, its gables decorated with stone foliage; it stands on columns whose capitals are also decorated with foliage scrolls (see photo overleaf). Melangell's relics were presumably removed from the grave in the eastern apse and placed inside the new, raised shrine, which appears to date from the mid-twelfth century. It may have been erected by Rhirid Flaidd (d. 1189), a local nobleman described as 'Proprietor of Pennant' in a poem by Cynddelw.[31] A solid Norman font also dates from this time.

Carved on the fifteenth-century rood screen, Prince Brochwel, with his huntsman and hounds, chases a hare into Melangell's lap. A quarter of a mile south of her chapel, rock steps in the valley side lead to a ledge known as 'Melangell's Bed'. To find Pennant Melangell, drive to Llangynog. As the B4391 passes the church, turn sharply up a signed single-track road to the head of the valley, until the road ends at the church.

Collen of Llangollen

Llangollen is named after St Collen. It is situated in the deep, narrow Dee valley, and was protected by the fort of Castell Dinas Brân, on a large conical hilltop to the north. The river broadens at Llangollen; it was unable to be bridged until John Trevor, later Bishop of St Asaph, built the first stone bridge over the Dee in about 1345 at Llangollen. This was considered to be a remarkable achievement; the antiquarian Daines Barrington, in a letter of 1770, refers to Llangollen Bridge as one of the 'five wonders of Wales'.[32]

Practically nothing is known about Collen. A sixteenth-century Welsh Life of Collen relates that he visited Cornwall and Glastonbury, and delivered people in the Vale of Llangollen from a fierce giantess by slaying her; this was a common metaphor for deliverance from paganism and conversion to Christianity. The church at nearby Rhuabon was formerly dedicated to Collen, while 20 miles to the south, Trallwm Collen ('Collen's marsh'), in the parish of Welshpool, and Castell Collen, in the parish of Llanfihangel Helygen in Radnor, are also named after him.[33] Collen may be commemorated at Colan in Cornwall and at Langolen in Finistère, Brittany.

There was probably a monastery at Llangollen, whose church housed a shrine to Collen. His tomb shrine (or *capel y bedd*), formerly known as the 'old church', stood to the west of the present church; it was demolished in the nineteenth century to create space for the current west tower. Fragments of the Romanesque stone shrine are built into the eastern wall of the vestry. Like that of Melangell, it was one of a number in this region, close to the English border, where Norman ecclesiastical influence was strong.[34] The core of the present church dates from the thirteenth century; both its nave and north aisle have a fine medieval hammerbeam roof.

St Derfel's Horse

Derfel is one of the lesser-known saints commemorated in the uplands of mid-Wales. Possibly a sixth-century monk of Breton origin, Derfel Gadarn ('the warrior') was said to have been a soldier before becoming a hermit at Llandderfel, 4 miles east-north-east of Bala. Llandderfel is on a valley slope, near the headwaters of the River Dee. Until the Reformation there was an ancient wooden statue in Llandderfel church depicting Derfel mounted on a horse, or possibly a red deer stag.

Thomas Cromwell, whom King Henry VIII made responsible for the confiscation of church property, sent agents throughout Britain to seize goods and 'abolish Popish practices'. There is a record of Cromwell's agent in Wales writing to his master in 1538 for instructions about Derfel's statue, because 'the people have so much trust in him that they

St Melangell's shrine, Pennant Melangell, Powys.

The River Dee at Llangollen, Denbighshire.

come daily on pilgrimage to him with cows or horses or money, to the number of five or six hundred on April 5th' (Derfel's feast day).[35]

Cromwell had the statue of Derfel brought to London to be burnt at Smithfield, but the rider's wooden mount can still be seen in the church porch. It stood in the chancel beside the communion table until 1730, when the rural dean, who disliked the presence of images in church, removed it and sawed off half of the animal's head. The wooden horse was still brought out each Easter Tuesday around the time of Derfel's feast, and carried in procession to the Wake Field, where it was fixed to a pole for children to ride.[36] Despite its damage through the centuries, the recumbent beast retains considerable character, with its deep eye sockets and most of a head half-turned over its right shoulder.

The small church has a magnificent oak rood screen, carved in about 1500. Llandderfel was sufficiently remote to remain a centre for Catholic worship; the last Mass in north Wales until recent times was celebrated here. The church is on a rise, near the end of the village. The key can be obtained from the former vicarage, now a nursing home, up the road, across from the church.

St Derfel's horse, Llandderfel, Gwynedd.

7

Beuno and Winifred

We learn about Beuno in a fourteenth-century Welsh version of a presumed lost Latin Life. This Middle Welsh text, *Buchedd Beuno*, was written in south Wales by a hermit at Llanddewi Brefi, in Ceredigion. In 1346 the anonymous hermit compiled an anthology of devotional readings that was apparently commissioned by his friend and patron, Gruffydd ap Llewelyn of Cantref Mawr. The book includes the Lives of David (translated from Rhygyfarch's Latin Life) and of Beuno, and a collection of medieval Welsh theological tracts.

The hermit begins his anthology by quoting from an early twelfth-century monk, Honorius Augustodunensis, who is thought to have lived as a hermit near the Irish monastery at Regensburg, in Bavaria. Honorius had written a book named *Elucidarium*, explaining in its prologue that he wished to elucidate, or throw light on subjects, while himself remaining anonymous, in order to prevent the jealousy of others. The hermit at Llanddewi Brefi felt a similar urge, and repeated the words of Honorius.[1] By quoting from this twelfth-century source, he also, incidentally, shows the breadth of his knowledge:

> This book is called Elucidarium, that is, a book that gives light; for in it light is thrown upon various dark subjects. I have not, however, revealed my own name lest these deeds should suffer through jealousy.[2]

The hermit at Llanddewi Brefi was writing at a time when the Normans had overrun much of Wales and the Welsh Church had been appropriated by the English. Llywelyn II had fallen, and future heroes such as Owain Glyndŵr had not yet appeared.[3] During this time of suffering and despair, the hermit chose to 'give light' by upholding David and Beuno as models for Welsh Christians; furthermore, he did so in their mother tongue. The Life describes how Beuno, who probably lived in the seventh century, was born of a noble family. He was educated at the monastery of Caerwent in south Wales by a holy man named Tangusius (probably Tathan, its founding saint). Here, Beuno 'learned the whole of the scriptures. Then, having learned the liturgy and rules of the church, he was ordained and became a priest'.[4]

We are told that Beuno founded churches in his native Powys and gathered a small group of disciples before leaving for Gwynedd, where he established churches at Holywell and Clynnog Fawr. The narrative corresponds to patterns of churches and wells dedicated to Beuno and his followers; it is likely to reflect the territorial interests and spiritual ties of the monastery at Clynnog Fawr, rather than historical fact.

Beuno's 'Magic' Powers

Writing at a time when the Welsh were disempowered, the author demonstrates Beuno's holiness through his power. Unlike the attributes of saints described in earlier Lives, Beuno's powers are depicted as magical, bardic qualities. The author portrays Beuno as a Christian healer, yet there are also pre-Christian echoes of the human head motif— three times, Beuno restores a severed head to its body. Early peoples believed that the head contained or controlled supernatural power, and Celtic warriors were known in the ancient world as head-hunters who displayed their trophies.[5]

Four times, Beuno curses someone who then dies; when the beautiful young Winifred flees from the lustful King Caradog, he cuts off her head with his sword at the church door, and the severed head rolls into the church. Beuno curses the king, who 'melted away into a lake, and was seen no more in this world'. He then placed the girl's head back on her body, covering it with his cloak while he celebrated Mass. After Mass, the girl arose healed, and was returned to her parents, like Jairus' daughter in the gospels (Mark 5. 21–43). Where her blood fell to the earth, a healing spring arose.

An echo of druidic religion and its association with oak trees may be preserved in the oak tree that Beuno plants over his father's grave which would kill an Englishman (or a pagan, in another version), but allow a Welshman to pass unharmed beneath its branches. Later legends recount that the trees which grew on his land were sacred to Beuno, who would injure or kill anyone who felled them. Beuno was nicknamed 'Dry Coat' (*Casul Sych*), after a magic coat that could never get wet, which Winifred wove for him each year, according to an anonymous Life of Winifred written in about 1135.[6]

Berriew

Beuno's Life relates that after his father's death, a local prince gave Beuno the small settlement of Berriew, five miles south-west of Welshpool, as a site for a monastery. Its name (*Aber Rhiw* in Welsh) indicates that Berriew grew beside the River Rhiw where it flows into the Severn, near the Roman road to Wroxeter. A pointed Bronze Age standing stone in Dyffryn Lane, a mile from the parish church is known as *Maen Beuno* (or 'Beuno's Stone'). This perhaps marked the settlement's holy place and here, according to local tradition, Beuno preached to the people (see photo on opposite page).

One day, when Beuno was at Berriew, out walking and examining his crops, he heard an Englishman on the other side of the Severn urging on his hunting dogs in his own language, calling, '*Kergia, Kergia!*' ('Charge! Charge!'). Beuno immediately returned to his disciples, told them to gather their belongings, and said they must leave because 'the race

Beuno's stone, Berriew, Powys.

of the foreigner whose voice he heard will overrun the place and they will possess it'.[7] In the face of the advancing English, he decided to move to safety, and travelled north-west through the Berwyn Mountains, into the valley of the River Dee.

There is a cluster of dedications to Beuno in the Dee valley around Gwyddelwern, on a Roman road 8 miles west of Llangollen. The Life recounts that Beuno founded a church here, and explains that its name derives from *Wyddel*, meaning 'Irishman'. This may indicate that it was settled by Irish immigrants. Outside the church, a magnificent yew tree dates from pre-Christian times (see colour plate 9). Beside the road, half a mile to the north, is the settlement's holy well. Older inhabitants remember this being the sole source of water for the village. People used to bathe in the well, believing in its miraculous powers, and water was taken to the church for baptisms.

Aberffraw, Anglesey

In the sixth century, Gwynedd was ruled by Maelgwyn, who had a stronghold on Anglesey. The *Life of Beuno* describes the saint coming to Maelgwyn's court at Aberffraw and, after restoring a man to life, being granted a plot of land. The parish church at Aberffraw is dedicated to Beuno. On the edge of the town, beside the medieval bridge over the tidal river (see colour plate 10), was Beuno's well; it stood in Malthouse Lane, between the river and the main road, but it was destroyed when the road was altered. Another church is dedicated to Beuno at nearby Trefdraeth. The Life describes Beuno travelling to Anglesey not across the Menai Strait but further south, landing in the shallow mud flats of Llanddwyn Island, near Newborough. From here, it was only a short journey to Aberffraw.

Clynnog Fawr

We are told that Beuno came to Caernarfon, where he asked the chieftain, Cadwallon, for a site on which to build a church. Cadwallon offered him land that belonged to someone else, after which Beuno cursed him. Cadwallon's cousin, Gwyddaint, then offered Beuno land in his own township of Clynnog, on the north coast of the Llŷn peninsula, ten miles south-west of Caernarfon.

According to the Life, using medieval legal language, Gwyddaint:

> …gave to God and Beuno his own inheritance, which is Clynnog, for all eternity without tax or tribute and with neither rights of possession nor any claim over it being held by any other person in the world.[8]

Beuno established his chief monastery here, where he spent the last phase of his life; he died at the end of Easter week, perhaps in the 650s.

The settlement became known as Clynnog Fawr ('Great holly place'), although holly does not grow much here. Perhaps it acquired its name from holly planted on the monastery's enclosure wall as extra protection, like the hedge of holly and hawthorn dating from the early seventh century, traces of which were found on the boundary earthworks at Iona.[9] Only the western half of the enclosure survives today, delineated in part by a stream flowing from Beuno's well. The well is 200 m south-west of the church, beside the main road. A flight of stone steps leads to a pool of clear water in a square well-house. It supplied water for the monastery, and became a famous healing well.

Beside the church, a small freestanding burial chapel (or *eglwys y bedd*) probably contained Beuno's relics. Until the eighteenth century, pilgrims came here to pray for healing. In 1914, restoration work in the chapel revealed a number of earlier stone foundations within the later sixteenth-century chapel. The foundations defined a rectangular structure, roughly half the size of the present chapel, situated at its centre; this is likely to have been where Beuno was buried. There were a number of slab-lined burials immediately to the south of the early chapel.[10]

The graves contained males—perhaps early monks—and another slab-lined grave was found in the corner, near a sundial that stands beside the outer wall of the chapel. The sundial is carved on the southern face of a pillar stone, pierced with a hole into which the gnomon was inserted to cast its shadow. Perhaps dating from the tenth century, this is one of Britain's earliest sundials; it would have been used by the monks in their ordered life of work and prayer. It was returned to the church after being used for other purposes on two different farms.

Above left: St Beuno's chapel, Clynnog Fawr, Gwynedd.

Above right: Celtic sundial, Clynnog Fawr, Gwynedd.

The impressive church beside the chapel was extended just before the Reformation to accommodate the crowds of pilgrims who came here to begin walking the Saints' Way, a route which led along the Llŷn peninsula to Bardsey Island at its tip. While Bangor was the most significant early monastery in Caernarvonshire, and the seat of an important bishopric, Clynnog was the other major monastery in this region, although it never became a bishop's see.

Clynnog was raided by the Vikings in 988, which suggests that it was worth plundering. It was also a focus for royal patronage; Gruffudd ap Cynan left money to Clynnog, and it appears to have received grants of land recorded in the *Book of St Beuno* (*Liber sancti Beugnobi*)—this was a gospel book which was extant at Clynnog in 1594. Quotations from one of its charters are included in a privilege of Edward IV.[11]

Inside Clynnog church is 'Beuno's chest', hollowed out from a single tree trunk; people put offerings into Beuno's chest to atone for crimes. Since Beuno's name means 'Knowing Cattle', they also offered money from the sale of animals that they considered to belong

Beuno's chest for offerings, Clynnog Fawr, Gwynedd.

to him. At birth, some Welsh calves and lambs have a slit in their ears known as 'Beuno's mark' (*Nôd Beuno*), as do Jersey cattle today. Until the late eighteenth century, farmers brought these animals to the churchwardens on the Sunday after Whitsun; they were sold, and the money was placed in the chest.[12]

Beuno's Church at Pistyll

Seven miles south-west of Clynnog Fawr, Beuno's tiny church at Pistyll is set in a sheltered hollow by the sea (see colour plate 11). At the east end of the hamlet of Pistyll, a steep track leads down from the main road to the church. The track is signed 'church', but the sign is visible only if one is travelling from the direction of nearby Nefyn. The church is set inside an oval Celtic enclosure, and built around the great boulder that was its original cornerstone. Ancient fruit bushes still grow in the churchyard, perhaps successors of those tended by medieval monks—gooseberry, daneberry, and sloes, and also hops and medicinal herbs.[13]

The font at Pistyll (see photo opposite) is decorated with a large interlaced ring-chain; it resembles several on Anglesey, including those at Trefdraeth and Llangristiolus. They are sometimes set against the west wall; some, like the font at Trefdraeth, have an area with little or no external carving, which suggests that they might have been carved after being placed in position.[14] They appear to be carved by local masons in an Irish-Norse style, which may be deliberately archaic. They are perhaps linked to the patronage of Gruffud ap Cynan (d. 1137) or his son, Owain Gwynedd (d. 1170).[15]

The church roof at Pistyll was thatched until the 1850s. One enters through a Romanesque arch, crossing the threshold—a corruption of 'the rush-hold', since it held strewn rushes inside the church. In earlier times, the earthen floor of a church was often spread with rushes and sweet-smelling herbs, and parishioners have revived this tradition.

Carved font, Pistyll, Gwynedd.

It is freshly strewn three times a year, at Christmas, Easter, and Lammas Day—which is the Sunday nearest 1 August. Its name derives from the Old English *hlaf-maesse*, or 'loaf Mass'. Lammas was the feast on which the bread for the Eucharist could first be made from the year's new corn, and loaves were offered in thanksgiving.

Pistyll is Welsh for 'waterfall', and beside the churchyard a fast-flowing stream tumbles into a large pool. This was the fishpond of the monastery that once stood on the site of Pistyll Farm, opposite the church. Pilgrims could rest at the monastery or at nearby farms, and many would sleep in shelters in the hospice field that adjoined the churchyard. There are similar hospice fields beside other churches on the Saints' Way that led along the Llŷn peninsula to Bardsey Island. At Pistyll, travellers could buy food and firewood from the villagers. They were entitled to ask for shelter, bread and cheese, in return for which the local inhabitants were excused from paying rent to their monastic landowners.[16]

Llanveynoe-under-Clodock

Far away from his Powys homeland, a church in south Wales is named Llanveynoe, or 'church of Beuno'. It is 25 miles north-west of Caerwent, so the author of Beuno's Life relates that after he left the monastery at Caerwent the local king, Ynyr Gwent, gave Beuno land at Llanveynoe-under-Clodock, 'together with all the people who lived on this land, and all their worldly goods'.[17]

This remote settlement is on a shoulder of the Black Mountains, 3 miles north-west of Clodock. The church is now dedicated to Saints Beuno and Peter; dedications to the apostles were often introduced in Norman times. A yew tree in the churchyard may predate the church. Inside are two fine tenth-century cross-slabs. One is engraved with a plain cross and the inscription 'HAESDUR FECIT CRUCEM' ('Haesdur made [this] cross'). On the other slab, a simple figure of Christ hangs from a cross; this may be the top of a coffin (see photo opposite). The present church was built in the thirteenth century; its walls and roof are of local sandstone. South of the church is a slender sandstone preaching cross. To find the church, drive north from Clodock through Longtown and turn left at the sign for Llanveynoe. After a mile, the small church is visible along a track to the left of the road, opposite a telephone kiosk.

Llanaelhaearn

This village is situated at the foot of Yr Eifl, a mountain at the neck of the Llŷn peninsula that is famous for its well-preserved Iron Age hilltop village. The settlement below, halfway between Beuno's churches of Clynnog and Pistyll, is named after Aelhaearn, who was said to be one of three brother monks who were followers of Beuno. A chapel was also dedicated to Aelhaearn near Beuno's church at Gwyddelwern.

Inside Llanaelhaearn church, set into the wall, is a sixth-century memorial stone inscribed in Latin: 'ALIORTUS ELMETIACO HIC IACET', or 'here lies Aliortus, [a man] from Elmet'. The gravestone was found in a field beside the churchyard named 'the Garden of the Saints'. Elmet was a distant Celtic kingdom around present-day Leeds.

A family from the Leeds area settling in the Llŷn peninsula must have been even more unusual in Celtic times than it would be today, giving rise to this unique early Christian epitaph. It hints at a group displaced from northern Britain in the face of Saxon conquest; early written sources preserve a similar tradition. In the churchyard, another Romano-Celtic grave marker commemorates a Christian named Melitus.

Cwyfan

Cwyfan was another disciple of Beuno; his church on a tidal islet at Llangwyfan (see colour plate 12), 2 miles west of Aberffraw, was described in Chapter 1. There are three more churches dedicated to Cwyfan, near to those of Beuno: one at Tudweiliog on the Llŷn peninsula; another at Llangwyfan, near Gwyddelwern; and a third at Dyserth, 3 miles south-east of Rhyl, near the north Welsh coast.

Cwyfan's church at Dyserth is at the foot of a high waterfall (see colour plate 13). The name Dyserth comes from the Latin word *desertum*—which, as we have seen, means 'an empty place'. This is the western equivalent of the Greek term *eremos* or 'hermitage', an ancient monastic word that was used by the monks and nuns who went into the deserts of Syria, Egypt and Palestine in search of a solitary place to pray.

European pilgrims were impressed by the wisdom and holiness of these Desert Mothers and Fathers, and wished to follow their example. Since there were no deserts in Britain, monks searched for a similar 'empty place' on a rocky headland or small island, or in a

Slab depicting the Crucifixion,
Llanveynoe under Clodock, Hereford
and Worcester.

Tombstone for a man who was from near Leeds, Llanaelhaearn, Gwynedd.

St Cwyfan's church, Llangwyfan, Anglesey.

remote valley. Scattered across Ireland, Scotland, and Wales are places named Dyserth, or Díseart in Irish. Each indicates an 'empty place' where a person could search for God in solitude.

Dyserth

Cwyfan or his unknown follower chose a magnificent location for his 'desert', within sight and sound of the waterfall's spray. At its foot, the pool provided water for drinking and washing, and a place in which to immerse candidates for baptism. Watercress, valued as food by Celtic monks, grows thickly in the cold stream flowing past the church.

Inside, the remains of two elaborate Celtic crosses indicate that a community continued on the site. One is first mentioned by the seventeenth-century antiquarian Edward Lhuyd as standing south of the church—he says that it may have functioned as a cross that denoted sanctuary (or *noddfa*). The base of a second cross was discovered when the church was being restored in the nineteenth century (see photo opposite).

Half a mile north-west of the church is Cwyfan's holy well, which is now dry. In the early twentieth century, people still fished for trout in the well.[18] Fish in wells were regarded with awe and respect, and were considered to bring healing.[19] To find the well, with the church on your right, continue along the road. Turn right at the main road; the well is soon visible, on the right.

Another cross is at some distance from the Dyserth. Now known as *Maen Achwyfan* ('Stone of lamentation'), it was originally named *Maen Machwyfan* ('Stone of Cwyfan's

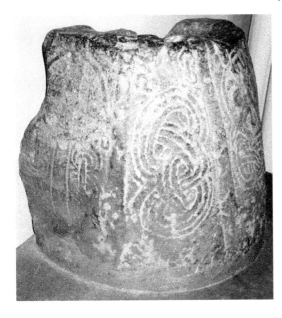

Left: Carved cross base, Dyserth, Denbighshire.

Below left: St Cwyfan's well, Dyserth, Denbighshire.

Below right: Stone of Cwyfan's field, at Dyserth parish boundary, Denbighshire.

field'). It is almost certainly still in its original position, 2.5 miles east of the settlement, on the parish boundary between Dyserth and Whitford; its name implies ownership of the land on which it stood.[20] The magnificent circle-headed cross in Viking style dates from the eleventh century, and is an example of Hiberno-Norse sculpture found around the Irish Sea. Examples of this type of cross are also found in Cheshire and Cumbria.[21]

St Winifred

Winifred lived in the mid-seventh century; her Welsh name, Gwenfrewi, means 'radiant Freda'. Her family home was said to have been at Holywell in Flintshire, which later came under the control of the English earldom of Chester. This may explain her English name and cult. Two Lives of Winifred survive—a *Vita prima* (c. 1135) written from a Welsh perspective, concludes with a collection of miracles worked long after her death, 'in the time of the French', when the Anglo-Normans conquered Flintshire. A *Vita secunda* was written a few years later for an English audience by Robert, Prior of Shrewsbury, after Winifred's relics were transferred to the abbey in 1138. Robert does not appear to have read the first Life of Winifred.

In the first Life, Winifred's story is presented against a twelfth-century political background, when the Welsh of Gwynedd attacked and re-conquered Flintshire for a time. One of the miracles in the first Life describes Winifred's delight that the French are expelled from Flintshire by the Welshmen of Gwynedd. There was now a new relationship between Holywell, the principal cult site of Flintshire, and Clynnog Fawr, a major church of Gwynedd, which Beuno appears to confirm when he leaves Holywell for Clynnog, and asks Winifred to make him a cloak. He says:

> My sister, God has appointed this place for you, and it is right that I should go somewhere else, where God will procure me somewhere to live. But every year, around this day, do this for me: send me a cloak made by your own labour.[22]

The first Life recounts that Winifred vowed virginity, and was educated by Beuno in the liberal arts (ch. 7); such an education is presented as normal for nuns. In return, Beuno received land on her father's estate, and he settled at Holywell. He also celebrated daily Mass for the family (ch. 7); his church is presented as a chapel on a nobleman's estate.[23] One day, when Winifred was taking fire (to burn incense) and salt water from her father's house for Sunday Mass (ch. 8), the local prince, Caradog ab Alog, tried to rape her. She fled to the church, where he cut off her head, to the dismay of Beuno and her parents:

> Perceiving this calamity, [Beuno] was enmeshed in very great grief and leaving the altar proceeded quickly to the door, desiring to know who had committed a murder of this sort. And his eyes being raised, he saw bloody Caradog still standing with his gory blade in hand, and understanding that the deed was done by Caradog he cursed him on that very spot. And immediately he melted in his presence, as wax before fire.[24]

Beuno healed Winifred, and where her head fell to the ground, Holywell's healing spring arose.

The hermit of Llanddewi Brefi incorporated the first Life of Winifred into his *Life of Beuno*, adding a new level of theological interpretation. In his account of Caradog murdering Winifred, she arises healed only at the end of Mass. The hermit uses phrases from the story of Jesus raising Lazarus from the dead in the Gospel of John (John 11. 1–45)—Beuno covers her over with his cloak until after Mass, when he removes the clothing (see John 11. 44). Many who had seen the miracle began to believe in Christ (see John 11. 46):

> Then Beuno took the girl's head and placed it back with the body, covering the body with his cloak and saying to her mother and father who were mourning for her: 'Be quiet for a little while and leave her until the Mass is over'. Then Beuno celebrated the sacrifice to God. When the Mass was finished, the girl rose up, entirely healed and dried the sweat from her face; God and Beuno healed her. Where her blood fell to the earth, a spring was formed, which even today still heals people and animals.... Many who had seen what had happened began to believe in Christ.[25]

The author presents the event as a death and resurrection that takes place in the context of the Mass, itself an enactment of Christ's death and resurrection. The event is seen not as a murder story, or even as a moral tale of the triumph of good over evil. Winifred offered her body as a sacrifice to God; her severed head, her body and blood, are separated like the body and blood of Jesus in the Mass, before she is resurrected by Beuno.

A saint's Life was read aloud at Mass on their feast day. Listening to the story in church, its Welsh hearers might recall the bloody death of their own relatives at the hand of the Anglo-Normans, and commend them to God, encouraged to believe in their resurrection—like that of Winifred and of Christ, whose death and resurrection they were gathered to celebrate. In this way, the hermit of Llanddewi Brefi transforms the story into a devotional meditation which was also intended to inspire hope in the hearts of its listeners.

Winifred's Well

According to her Life, Winifred established a convent of nuns at Holywell, where her healing spring attracted pilgrims. Successive English kings honoured Winifred; King Henry V walked from Shrewsbury to Holywell in 1416 to give thanks for his success at the Battle of Agincourt.[26] Pilgrims could bathe in a rectangular pool; in the chapel roof, a corbel depicts a medieval pilgrim carrying a sick man on his shoulders, to immerse him in the water. The present chapel, with its star-shaped pool over the spring, was commissioned by Margaret Beaufort in 1483.

After the Reformation, pilgrims flocked to Holywell in spite of persecution by anti-Catholic authorities. Jesuit priests lived here in hiding and secretly celebrated Mass in the town's inns. A Jesuit named John Gerard described his pilgrimage to Holywell in 1593:

St Winifred's well, Holywell, Flintshire.

Ancient landing stage at Holywell,
Flintshire.

Once I was there on November 3, St Winifred's feast…. There was a hard frost at the time, and though the ice in the stream had been broken by people crossing it the previous night, I still found it very difficult to cross with my horse the next morning. But frost or no frost, I went down into the well like a good pilgrim. For a quarter of an hour I lay down in the water and prayed. When I came out, my shirt was dripping, but I kept it on and pulled all my clothes back over it, and was none the worse for my bathe.[27]

In the eighteenth century, groups of pilgrims from Lancashire crossed the River Mersey by ferry and then walked up over the Wirral. They waited for low tide and crossed the treacherous sands of the Dee estuary on foot. Eventually, they climbed the narrow valley to St Winifred's well. On their return journey, they lit beacons on the Wirral to signal for a boat to ferry them north again.[28] In 1870 the town council opened a hospice for pilgrims; many continue to come for healing.

Bodfari

A church is dedicated to Winifred at Gwytherin in Conwy, and the second Life recounts her journey to Gwytherin, describing the locations where she stayed with her nuns along the way. She travelled 7 miles inland to the church of a monk named Deifor at Bodfari. The settlement's name derives from *Bod Deifor*, or 'Deifor's dwelling'. Deifor's church (see colour plate 14) is on the side of a hill above the Roman road from Chester to Caerhun, which was a fort guarding the River Conwy; there was a Roman station at Bodfari, and a small settlement. The Normans rededicated Deifor's church to St Stephen.

A thirteenth-century manuscript mentions Deifor's well, which was opposite the Roman station, at the foot of the hill. Even after the Reformation, villagers went in procession from the church down to the well, where the litany, the Ten Commandments, the epistle, and gospel were read. The poorest person in the parish offered a chicken after walking nine times round the well—a cock for a boy or a pullet for a girl. Children were also 'dipped to the neck at three of its corners, to prevent their crying at night'.[29] By the 1950s the well was dry, but there was still a tap, and seats round the well.[30]

Henllan

The Life relates that after leaving Bodfari, Winifred travelled south-west for another 7 miles until she reached the church of Sadwrn at Henllan. Sadwrn is the Welsh form of the Latin name Saturninus, which possibly suggests an early saint. Henllan church is set on a hilltop at a crossroads. As we have seen, its name means 'old' or 'former' church—it can refer to a church which fell into disuse, but was later rebuilt.

The large fourteenth-century church that can be seen today is built on sloping ground above a stream, on the site of a smaller, earlier church, from which the font and a single pillar have been preserved; they are in the churchyard, near the porch. The embattled fourteenth-century tower (see colour plate 15) stands on a rock, south-east of the church; this was probably to avoid adding its considerable weight to the church, which may have been considered to be on insecure ground on the hillside. The tower retains its original oak door.

There are two churches named Llansadwrn that possibly refer to the same saint, one in Carmarthenshire and another on Anglesey, 3 miles west of Beaumaris. At Llansadwrn in Anglesey, Sadwrn's unique tombstone, dating from about 530, was formerly in the churchyard and is now set in the chancel wall. It is carved in Roman capitals, and reads: 'HIC BEATUS SATURNINUS SE[PULTUS] IACIT ET SUA S[ANCTA] CONIUX. PAX [VOBISCUM SIT]', or 'Here lies blessed Saturninus and his saintly wife. Peace be with you both' (see photo opposite).

Gwytherin

The Life describes Winifred continuing to the remote settlement of Gwytherin, 12 miles south of Colwyn Bay, in the valley of the River Cledwyn. At Gwytherin a monk named Eleri had founded a small monastery; his mother, Theonia, was its first leader, and she was succeeded by Winifred. In his *Life of Wenefred*, Robert, Prior of Shrewsbury, indicates that Gwytherin was the site of her grave, but that her relics had recently been transferred to the Benedictine abbey. According to Robert, the community 'frequently lamented to each other that they had a great need of some relics of the saints, and with all their efforts applied their minds to acquiring some'.

Gwytherin is an ancient site; the church is situated above what may be a burial mound, between a pair of yew trees approximately 2,000 years old, planted on an east-west axis, aligned with the rising and setting sun.[31] Alternatively, the small-but-pronounced promontory on which the church is built, with steep slopes to the north, south, and east, has been interpreted as a possible Iron Age promontory fort.[32]

The churchyard was larger than it is today; it included Winifred's *capel y bedd*, or chapel of her grave. The seventeenth-century antiquarian Edward Lhuyd wrote that it was still standing; it was demolished early in the following century.[33] Beside the church is a row of four small standing stones. In the fifth or sixth century, one of these was used as a tombstone by a Christian family, for inscribed on it in Latin is '[The stone of] Vinnemaglus, son of Senemaglus' (see photo on p. 120).

Winifred's Shrine

Winifred is said to have died at Gwytherin, and her remains were enshrined in a wooden reliquary which may have survived until the mid-nineteenth century. In around 1690, Edward Lhuyd made a careful drawing of it—he depicts a house-shaped shrine with a triangular cross-section and short supporting legs. It appears to be decorated by three circular medallions with metal strips and perhaps metal sheets, surmounted by a small cross.

Memorial to Sadwrn and his wife at Llansadwrn, Anglesey.

Four pre-Christian standing stones, Gwytherin, Conwy.

Christian inscription on an earlier stone, Gwytherin, Conwy.

The casket's decorative roundels resemble eighth- and early ninth-century Anglo-Saxon metalwork; it is uncertain whether the shrine was created in England, Ireland or Wales.

The shrine may have contained small relics of Winifred such as bone fragments, teeth or *bandea* (pieces of cloth which had touched her body).[34] In 1991, one the shrine's oak gable ends, with the remains of its copper-alloy rivets still in place, was discovered in the Catholic church at Holywell.[35] The shrine was probably almost 40 cm long and 30 cm high. Its shape and form recall St Manchán's shrine, which was recovered from a bog at Lemanaghan in Offaly, 12 miles east of Clonmacnoise. This magnificent Irish shrine has been dated to around 1130 (see photo opposite).

There appears to have been a flourishing monastery at Gwytherin in medieval times; it may have been a double community for both monks and nuns. *The Survey of the Honour of Denbigh* (1334) states that there were *abbates* ('abbots') at Gwytherin who were supported by bond under-tenants. Bond tenants and their heirs could not leave their land, which suggests that there had been a stable community at Gwytherin for a considerable length of time. The survey of 1334 describes Gwytherin as largely owned by 'abbots of the lineage of Cynon ap Llywarch'; it appears that by this time Gwytherin had become, in effect, a family monastery.[36]

Gwytherin's little church was thoroughly restored in the nineteenth century, but a medieval grave slab inscribed with a cross is set in the chancel step. The church contains a medieval tub font and a chest for offerings to Winifred's shrine, carved from a single tree trunk, similar to that of Beuno at Clynnog Fawr.

St Manchán's shrine, Lemanaghan, Offaly, Ireland.

St Winifred's Well, Woolston

Woolston is a small Shropshire village 3 miles south-east of Oswestry; Winifred's well in Woolston may commemorate a stage in the progress of her relics from Gwytherin to Shrewsbury. From Woolston it would have been a day's journey to Shrewsbury. The water flows through stone troughs to create pools for bathing (see colour plate 16); it healed wounds, bruises, and broken bones. People with eye diseases visited a spring lower down the water course.[37]

The site may have been a medieval moot where people gathered to administer justice, for a courthouse is built over the well, dating from the sixteenth or seventeenth century. It is a charming half-timbered building in a secluded copse at the end of a leafy lane. In early times, gatherings to enact laws were held at a significant site such as a mound or a standing stone, a holy well, or an ancient oak tree.

To find the well, coming from Oswestry, turn left into the village and, as the road bends right, walk left down a lane marked 'access to houses only'. At the end of the track, the footpath to the well is through a gate on the right. While Winifred's shrine at Holywell is seldom without pilgrims, her well at Woolston is rarely visited.

Anglesey and the Menai Strait: Deiniol, Cybi and Seiriol

In this chapter we will focus on early Christians living on both sides of the Menai Strait. On the mainland, there were settlements at Caernarfon, near the south-western end of the Menai Strait, and at Bangor, towards its north-eastern end. There were also Christian communities on Anglesey. While there were many Irish Christians in south Wales, this was less common in the north. There are few stones inscribed in Irish ogham in north-west Wales; most are in the south. However, there are about fifty tombstones carved in Roman Gallic style in the north, including four of the earliest. This suggests that the Church in north Wales from the fifth to the seventh centuries was influenced by the Church of Gaul.

Tombstones at Penmachno

At Penmachno, 22 miles south-east of Caernarfon, three pillar stones provide evidence of early Christian life in this region. The inscription on one fifth-century stone reads: 'Cantiorix lies here. He was a citizen of Venedos, cousin of Maglos the magistrate'. The term *Venedos* is a Latin form of 'Gwynedd'—it demonstrates that this area was recognised as a region by the fifth century. The typically Roman terms 'citizen' and 'magistrate' (*civis* and *magistratus*) occur in no other British Christian inscription; they imply that there was a formal Roman system of government in this area. Perhaps administration in the Roman style continued in fifth-century Gwynedd, possibly based on the Roman fort at Caernarfon.[1]

Another fifth-century pillar is carved with a chi-rho symbol for Christ, above an inscription which reads in translation: 'Carausius lies here in this heap of stones'. Carausius is an uncommon name; it may have become fashionable in the late third century, when an emperor of that name ruled Britain as a breakaway state from Rome. The self-styled emperor was prominent in Wales, with which he may have had some link, since hoards that contain coins bearing his name are common in Wales.[2] The 'heap of stones' describes a burial cairn, which was a way of marking an important grave.

A third slab is inscribed: 'The stone of […], son of Avitorius. Set up in the time of the consul Justinus'. This consul held office in 540; he can be identified from inscriptions in the Lyons district of France. The tombstone suggests a link between Gaul and Gwynedd in the sixth century.[3] Penmachno is 3 miles south of Betws-y-Coed; it is signposted south from the A5, and is at the end of the B4406. The church is locked; the key is at the nearby farmhouse.

Caernarfon

The Roman fortress of Segontium, now on the eastern edge of Caernarfon, was built in AD 77. For 300 years, until 394, it was the military and administrative centre of north-west Wales; up to 1,000 soldiers were stationed there. Close to the fort is a church dedicated to a saint named Peblig; his Latin name, Publicus, suggests that he was a Romanised Christian. The church may be on the site of a Roman cemetery attached to the fort; a Roman altar can be seen in the churchyard.

The church dates from the fourteenth century, with a sixteenth-century tower and chapel. *The Llanbeblig Book of Hours* survives from the fourteenth century; this is a devotional manuscript of prayers based upon the monastic office, for use at home by a noble Caernarfon family. It is now in the National Library of Wales. Llanbeblig church is on the A4085 Portmadoc Road, on the same side of the road as the Roman fort, a little lower down the hill.

According to a thirteenth-century text, *The Dream of Maxen Wledig*, which is thought to have originated in the eleventh century, Magnus Maximus, the self-styled emperor of Britain, Gaul and Spain from 383 to 388, married a princess of Caernarfon named Elen

St Peblig's church, Llanbeblig, Gwynedd.

Luyddoc.[4] This is now considered unlikely, but Maximus and Elen are named in early Welsh genealogies. Although his time in Britain was short, Magnus Maximus features in medieval Welsh texts. He is mentioned by the *Historia Brittonum*, written in around 828, and in the thirteenth-century *Triads of the Island of Britain*.[5] He is a key figure in one of the branches of the Mabinogion, *The Dream of Maxen Wledig*.[6]

In these traditions, Magnus Maximus is linked with the final withdrawal of Roman troops from Britain, although this took place twenty years after his death; he is also associated with the early British settlement of Brittany.[7] His name is found in a lengthy inscription on the ninth-century Pillar of Eliseg at Valle Crucis, which will be described in the next chapter.

Migration from the North

North Wales also differs from the south in that there was considerable movement of people from northern England and southern Scotland into north Wales from the second century BC to the seventh century AD. Towards the end of the Roman occupation, in the late fourth century, the Romans reorganised the northern frontier of Britain and deported some of the population of Northumbria and the Firth of Forth to north Wales, perhaps to protect British territory against Irish raiders. Early genealogists called the northerners the Sons of Cunedda, after an ancestral chieftain; a number of north Welsh saints are described as descendants of Cunedda.

Cunedda's people made their headquarters at Aberffraw on Anglesey. Other northerners migrated southwards and settled among the people of Cunedda. In the previous chapter, we examined the sixth-century tombstone of a northerner who came from near Leeds, at Llanaelhaearn, on the Llŷn peninsula. Among the people of Cunedda was Maelgwyn Gwynedd, a sixth-century Christian prince of Strathclyde who left home, possibly for political reasons, and carved out a territory in the land annexed by the Sons of Cunedda. He came to rule much of north Wales from Aberffraw.

King Pabo

According to Welsh genealogies, among the immigrants from north Britain was King Pabo, who fled south with his wife after being defeated in battle by the Picts. King Cyngen of Powys received them kindly, and their friendship was consolidated by a royal marriage; Pabo's daughter, Arddun, married Cyngen's son and successor, Brochmael. Pabo is thought to have given his name to Llanbabo church (see colour plate 17) above Lake Alaw, in the centre of northern Anglesey. The settlement is now deserted; a few ruined cottages surround the small church, which dates from the fourteenth century.

At this time a grave slab was carved in low relief with an effigy of Pabo portrayed as a medieval monarch. He wears an elegant full-length tunic; a crown and sceptre indicate his royal status. Around the edge of the tombstone, most of a Latin inscription survives, which has been translated as: 'Here lies Pabo, Pillar of the Britons, Confessor. Gruffudd ab Ithel offered [this] image'. The inscription uses the ancient title Pabo Post Pryden— 'Post' meaning 'pillar' and 'Pryden' meaning 'Britain'. However, since the tombstone is of late date, it has been suggested that the church might be dedicated to a different Pabo.

Bangor Is-coed

We are informed that Pabo's son, Dunod, became a monk—in Latin, his name is Donatus, meaning 'Given [to God]'. He is said to have founded a large monastery beside the River Dee, 4 miles south-east of Wrexham, at Bangor Is-coed ('Bangor under the woods'). Bede describe's Cyngen's son, Brochmael, as the monks' protector (*defensor*). The monastery is thought to have been somewhere between the present village and the racecourse a mile to the south-west. In 731 Bede called it the 'most noble monastery' of the Britons, and wrote:

> There were so many monks that they were divided into seven groups, each with its own superior. Each group contained no fewer than three hundred men, who all lived by the work of their own hands.[8]

The flat, fertile plain of the River Dee provided the farmland necessary to support such a large community. It seems to have been a complex institution, which, in addition to monks, housed bishops and 'learned men', as well as a hermit. Presumably it was well-endowed with land, perhaps by Brochmael.[9]

In about 615 the Saxon King Ethelfrith of Northumbria attacked and defeated the King of Powys, Brochmael's grandson, in a battle near Bangor Is-coed. The monks climbed a nearby hill to pray for victory, but many of them were also slaughtered. Bede describes how King Ethelfrith had no pity on them, while Brochmael failed to act as the monks' *defensor*. Praying against one's enemies was then considered a serious task:

> Many of [the monks], having observed a fast of three days, resorted among others to pray at the aforesaid battle, having one Brochmael appointed for their protector, to defend them whilst they were intent upon their prayers, against the swords of the barbarians. King Ethelfrith being informed of the occasion of their coming, said, 'If then they cry to their God against us, in truth, though they do not bear arms, yet they fight against us, because they oppose us by their prayers.'
>
> He, therefore, commanded them to be attacked first, and then destroyed the rest of the impious army, not without considerable loss of his own forces. About twelve hundred of those that came to pray are said to have been killed, and only fifty to have escaped by flight.[10]

By the twelfth century, the monastery was a large ruin. In the thirteenth century, a new church was built of red sandstone, with a fine east window. Around the same time, a packhorse bridge was built beside the churchyard (see colour plate 18). The River Dee is so broad at this point that it could be crossed only by boat before that time. The sole reminder of the Celtic monastery is a carved slab 3 metres long, decorated with curving tendrils. It was part of a high cross, and was found in a field a few hundred metres upstream from the church. It can now be seen beside the chancel step.

Deiniol of Bangor

We are told that Deiniol (or Daniel in English) was a son of Dunod. A number of churches in north Wales are dedicated to Deiniol, who is first recorded in the early ninth-century Irish *Martyrology of Tallaght*. His importance at this early date is demonstrated by the fact that he is one of only three Welsh saints recorded in the martyrology.

The tenth-century *Annales Cambriae* gives the date of his death as 584, and calls him 'Daniel of the Bangors'.[11] This suggests that he was already known as the patron of both Bangor Is-coed and Bangor on the Menai Strait. In 1620, a *Cae Ffynnon Daniel* ('Field of Daniel's well') was recorded at Bangor Is-coed. The earliest accounts of Deiniol's life are a praise poem written by Dafydd Trefor in 1520, and short readings for his feast, copied by the antiquarian Thomas Wiliems between 1594 and 1610. According to these late sources, he was a hermit near Pembroke before he became a bishop.[12]

Deiniol is chiefly associated with Bangor beside the Menai Strait. The noun *bangor* means 'the binding part of a wattle fence'; the site was enclosed by driving posts into the ground and weaving branches between them. Thus the monastery took its name from its surrounding palisade; there was another Bangor beside Belfast Lough in northern Ireland. Deiniol's church became a cathedral at the centre of one of Britain's earliest dioceses.

An oval enclosure to the east of Bangor cathedral, on the south-east bank of the River Adda, is visible on John Speed's map of Bangor (1610), and is likely to be the location of Deiniol's monastery. South of the medieval cathedral, the line of the present day High Street also perpetuates the enclosure's boundaries. In 1984–5, an area of 450 square metres was excavated here at Berllan Bach. The earliest features of the site were seventy-eight graves, most of them aligned with the cathedral or facing east.[13]

Some of the graves were cut by a rectangular ditch, the lowest fills of which produced material radiocarbon dated to AD 680–990 and AD 893–1160. The ditch suggests a change of use for this part of the site, which later contained a medieval chantry chapel, Capel Gorfyw; this eventually became a tithe barn.[14]

The monastery was destroyed by the Vikings in 1073; all that remains are fragments of stone sculptures with geometric carvings. These are thought to have been created in the eleventh or twelfth century, in an archaic style. The presence of what appears to be a socket on one stone suggests that it may have held a wooden fitting, perhaps a screen.[15]

A church and holy well on Anglesey are named after Deiniol's son at Llanddaniel Fab, or 'church of Daniel the Younger'; it is first mentioned in a document of 1475. The village lies just south of the Holyhead Road, 2 miles from the Menai Strait. Unlike Deiniol's

Anglesey: sites described in the text·

Church of Daniel the Younger, Llanddaniel Fab,
Anglesey.

magnificent fourteenth-century cathedral, his son's church is hidden behind a row of houses in the village that bears his name.

Anglesey

By the sixth century, the names of several Welsh kingdoms are recorded, including Gwynedd, where a dynasty seems to have been established by Maelgwyn, who is mentioned by Gildas in the sixth century. A ninth-century document entitled *Historia Brittonum* ('*History of the Britons*') describes Maelgwyn as 'a great king'. Anglesey was the island stronghold of this kingdom, which appears to have been a powerful one; its chief court was at Aberffraw, and Anglesey remained the centre of the kingdom until the later thirteenth century.[16]

Maelgwyn's line came to an end in the early ninth century; his successors expanded the kingdom until they not only controlled the former counties of Caernarvonshire, Denbighshire, and Merioneth, but at times became overlords of most of Wales, especially under Rhodri Mawr (who ruled 844–78) and Gruffud ap Llywelyn (1039–63).[17]

Llangadwaladr: A Royal Burial Ground

Llangadwaladr is 2 miles east of Aberffraw; it was originally named *Eglwys Ail*, or 'wattle church'. The name *Eglwys* derives from the Latin *ecclesia* ('church'), and can refer to an early foundation, while *Ail* describes a wooden construction. The name *Eglwys Ail* was first recorded in 1254; it was gradually superseded by Llangadwaladr, or church of Cadwaladr, a name first found in 1508.[18]

The church appears to have been used as a burial site by the early kings of Gwynedd, who lived at Aberffraw. A memorial stone dating from the mid-seventh century was discovered near the church, and is now set into the wall above the south doorway. The stone is carved in a mixture of Roman capitals and half-uncial script, and incised with a small cross; it reads 'CATAMANUS REX SAPIENTIS[S]SIMUS OPINATIS[S]IMUS OMNIUM REGUM', or '[the memorial to] King Catamanus, wisest [and] most renowned of all kings'.

Catamanus may be identified with Cadfan, King of Gwynedd (d. 645), one of the Sons of Cunedda. The stone may not have been erected on his death, however, since the church was probably founded by his grandson Cadwaladr (d. 664), who may then have commissioned the monument.[19] The inscription is phrased in the style of the imperial court at Constantinople, and the lettering is in the latest European style.

Cadwaladr is described in Welsh sources as a prayerful, peace-loving man, the son of King Cadwallon. He was nicknamed 'the Battleshunner', but despite this, together with King Penda of Mercia, Cadwaladr defeated and killed King Edwin of Northumbria in 633. He later led his people against the army of the King of Wessex, and suffered a grave defeat at Peonne in Somerset in 658. Two other churches in Denbighshire and Monmouthshire are dedicated to Cadwaladr. The earliest structural features of his church on Anglesey are a Norman doorway and a twelfth-century window.

Llanfair Pwyllgwyngyll

Ten miles east of Llangadwaladr is Llanfair Pwllgwyngyll, whose full name reads in translation: 'Church of St Mary by the pool with the white hazels, near the fierce whirlpool by the church of St Tysilio, near the red cave'. The church of St Tysilio is the chapel on Llandysilio Island, which was described in Chapter 6, and the fierce whirlpool is the Swellies beyond them. However, the extension to the settlement's name was devised only in the 1860s, in order to attract tourism.

This remained a rural settlement within the kingdom of Gwynedd; in 1563, there were only about eighty persons living here. The church was heavily restored in the nineteenth century; excavations in 1847 revealed an apse in which the altar may formerly have stood, before the construction of the chancel in later medieval times.

A tenth-century ringed pin was found in the churchyard while digging a grave in 2005; this was a pin with a loose swivel ring inserted into a looped head. It was a form of dress fastener which became popular in Ireland. When Vikings settled in Ireland in the second half of the ninth century, they adopted the ringed pin as a form of jewellery. The example discovered at Llanfair Pwyllgwyngyll has a large, cube-shaped head; its shaft is decorated with a step pattern, while its ring is missing.[20]

Several similar pins have been found in Dublin, and they are widely distributed elsewhere; one example was discovered in a Norse grave in the Faroe Islands. Since the pin at Llanfair Pwyllgwyngyll was found in the cemetery, it may have been used to fasten a shroud.[21] It provides evidence for Irish-Norse culture around the Irish Sea during the tenth century, and suggests that a Christian Viking family might have lived here.

Vikings on Anglesey

In the ninth and tenth centuries, Wales was attacked by Vikings, as was most of northern Europe. Vikings first began to raid Wales in the mid-ninth century, when they killed King Cyngen of Powys and attacked the fertile land of Anglesey, with fleets based in Dublin, Limerick and the Isle of Man. After initially resisting these attacks, Rhodri Mawr was forced to flee to Ireland. Raids intensified in the later tenth century: the monastery at Caer Gybi (Holyhead) was attacked in 961, the royal stronghold at Aberffraw in 968, and the monastery at Penmon in 971. In 987 the Vikings are said to have killed 1,000 men and carried off 2,000 captives as slaves.

At the end of the tenth century they were expelled from Dublin, and they may have settled for a short time on Anglesey before proceeding to Chester. At the farmstead of Llanbedrgoch (or 'St Peter's red church'), 6 miles north-west of Llanfair Pwyllgwyngyll, objects including a ringed pin, a buckle, an iron knife blade and lead weights indicate a Viking presence. There is little evidence of Vikings elsewhere in Wales.

The settlement at Llanbedrgoch, on the flat coastal plain of eastern Anglesey, was discovered in 1994; excavation continued at the site until 2001. A small wattle-and-daub roundhouse and a large timber hall were built here some time between the fifth and the ninth century, and a massive enclosure wall was built around the settlement, perhaps in the time of Rhodri Mawr or his sons, to protect it from Norse invaders. The community was at its most prosperous in the tenth century, growing crops and herding livestock; craftsmen worked here and had contact with Viking merchants.[22]

With the development of maritime commerce, Llanbedrgoch appears to have become a trading post. It is not known whether Norsemen raided and captured the settlement or whether they integrated with the native Welsh, nor is it known if Vikings resided here; the site was no longer in use by the twelfth century. It had grown to prominence as trade developed between the Viking dominated cities of Dublin and Chester, leading to a more peaceful relationship with local peoples. Irish-Norse fleets were used by Welsh rulers as late as 1138 to fight the Normans in Ceredigion.

Cybi

Cybi is one of a group of Welsh saints whose Lives are to be found in a manuscript compiled around AD 1200, which combines legend and folklore with a limited amount of fact.[23] According to his Life, Cybi was born in Cornwall and travelled around the Irish Sea before reaching north-west Wales, landing on Anglesey. We are told that Cybi was the son of a Cornish chieftain; two churches in Cornwall are dedicated to him. One is at Tregony on the south coast; this was formerly a port in the tidal estuary of the River Fal. The other is at Duloe, 4 miles south of Liskeard.

According to Cybi's Life, Maelgwyn Gwynedd gave him permission to build a church in a fort at Holyhead, or Caer Gybi, in the north-east corner of Holy Island (also known as Ynys Cybi), which is connected to Anglesey by a causeway. The small Roman fort at Caer Gybi may have been constructed to repel Irish raiders, who attacked the west coast of Wales from the later third century onwards, before they subsequently settled in Anglesey and west Wales in the fifth century.

The fourth-century fort may have been no more than a fortified landing place, and the church sits neatly inside it, well protected by its Roman enclosure wall with towers at each corner. The earliest documentary evidence relating to the church refers to the Viking raid on Caer Gybi in 961, mentioned above; it suggests the presence of a monastery worth plundering. The present church dates from the thirteenth century. It was rebuilt in the late fifteenth and early sixteenth centuries; its elaborate porch contains fine carved stonework and a fan-vaulted roof.

In the south-west corner of the churchyard is a second building—the *eglwys y bedd*, or chapel of Cybi's shrine. It dates from the fourteenth century and may have housed Cybi's relics; a fifteenth-century poem describes a staff associated with Cybi at Caer Gybi. Excavation in 1992 identified the footings of an earlier, possibly twelfth-century building. The chapel's chancel was demolished in 1832, when evidence was found of at least one burial inside the chapel, and early medieval long-cist graves outside it, to the south, inside the fort.[24]

An Anglo-Saxon penny of Edward the Martyr (975–8) was found close to the inside face of the fort wall, a short distance from its north-west corner. The coin may have been

St Cybi's church (right) and burial chapel (left), inside a Roman fort, Caer Gybi, Anglesey.

an offering to the church, or may indicate a market controlled by the church.[25] There was formerly a holy well dedicated to Cybi, outside the fort to the north-east, at the junction of St Cybi Street and Cybi Place. It was frequently visited in the eighteenth century, and could still be seen a century later.

Cybi's Well on the Llŷn Peninsula

At Llangybi on the Llŷn peninsula, 6 miles north-east of Pwllheli, a remarkable medieval well house survives. It is situated at the edge of a wood in a small valley, 500 metres from the church named after Cybi; it is one of the most elaborate structures of its kind in this area of north Wales, although the present well house may date from no earlier than the twelfth or thirteenth century.

On the north side of the valley are two well chambers, adjoining a custodian's cottage built in about 1750. In the larger well chamber, closest to the cottage, steps lead down into the water from a surrounding ledge or paved walk. The dry stone walls are built of large blocks of stone, and there are five niches for seats in the walls. There is a lintel over the doorway, and the upper courses of masonry are overhanging, which suggests that the original builders had intended to construct a corbelled roof over the well (see photo overleaf).[26]

The smaller well chamber also contains a square pool surrounded by a ledge, with steps leading down into the water. To approach the well, pilgrims used two stone causeways across the waterlogged field; on the far side of the field there is an eighteenth-century toilet

St Cybi's well, Llangybi,
Gwynedd.

block. An eel lived in the well, where the patient stood barelegged; if the eel coiled itself round the patient's legs, it was believed that a cure would follow.[27]

The spring water possesses mineral properties, and cured a wide variety of illnesses. A register of cures made in 1766 describes how a man who had been blind for thirty years bathed his eyes for three consecutive weeks and recovered his sight. In the eighteenth century, seven people were cured of blindness caused by smallpox. The lame came to Llangybi on crutches, or were wheeled to the well in barrows. When they were cured, they gratefully left their crutches and barrows around the well, where they were noted by an observer in the early eighteenth century. Water was carried away in casks and bottles for use as medicine.[28]

A band of smugglers returning from a night's work with barrels of spirits explained when challenged by an excise officer that the casks contained water from Ffynnon Gybi! Until the eighteenth century, the church contained a chest, *Cyff Cybi*, for thank-offerings from pilgrims cured at the well. Cybi also has dedications at Llangybi-on-Usk north-east of Newport, and at Llangybi north-east of Lampeter in Ceredigion, where another healing well is named after him.

St Patrick's Church, Llanbadrig

There are a number of saints whose cult is local to Anglesey. Llanbadrig on the north coast of Anglesey, fifteen miles north-east of Caer Gybi, is probably dedicated not to the Irish Patrick but to Padrig ap Alfryt; he is first mentioned in a document from around 1250. He has been equated with a Bishop Patrick who fostered the Norseman Örlygur Hrappsson in the early ninth century. The Norseman is described in the *Landnámabák* (or *Book of Settlements*), a late thirteenth-century account of Viking settlements in Iceland which were established between the ninth and eleventh centuries. We are told that Hrappsson was among those who migrated from the Hebrides to Iceland; he invited Patrick to accompany him, but the bishop declined.[29]

Llanbadrig church is on a cliff top; half a mile out to sea is a rocky islet named *Ynys Badrig* ('Patrick's Isle'). On the mainland, a cave with a freshwater well, halfway up the cliff, is also named after him. The medieval church contains a stone slab decorated with carvings of a palm tree and two crossed fishes. They symbolise Christ, for the Greek letters which spell the word 'fish' form the first letters of the title 'Jesus Christ, Son of God, Saviour'. The palm represents a tree of life; the stone may date from the ninth to the eleventh century.

Carved pillar stone showing a fish and a palm tree, Llanbadrig, Anglesey.

There is a twelfth-century font in the church, which was rebuilt in the fourteenth and sixteenth centuries. A number of local landmarks are named after Patrick, including *Dinas Padrig* ('Patrick's fort'), *Pen Padrig* ('Patrick's hill'), *Rhos Padrig* ('Patrick's headland'), and *Porth Padrig* ('Patrick's harbour'). An atlas of Anglesey, *Atlas Môn* (published by Melville Richards in 1923), indicates a nearby site named *Tref Was Padrig*, or 'township of Patrick's servant'.[30] The dedication of the church may be seen in the context of a Viking presence on Anglesey. To find Llanbadrig, take the A5025 east from Cemais; at Neuadd, follow the track to the left, down to the cliffs.

Llaneilian

Llaneilian is a village on the north-east coast of Anglesey, 6 miles east of Llanbadrig and 1 mile east of Amlwch. Eilian is first mentioned in a document dating from around 1300; his popularity in medieval times arose largely from his supposed power of cursing his enemies. He was said to be a monk from Anglesey who cured Maelgwyn Gwynedd's father, Cadwallon, of blindness. In return for being cured, Cadwallon gave Eilian a grant of land to build a church at what was later named Llaneilian. According to the legend, Cadwallon gave him as much land as his tame doe could cross in a day, but a rich person's greyhound killed the doe, and was cursed by Eilian.

There may have been a community of clergy living here, since there is a thirteenth-century reference to its abbot's property (or *abadaeth* in Welsh). The church dates from the fifteenth century, with a fourteenth-century chancel, from which a stone passage leads to Eilian's chapel—a small room measuring 4.5 by 3.5 metres. The chapel was formerly separate from the church itself; it was known as *Myfyr Llaneilian* or *Myfyr Eilian*, at least since 1696. The word *Myfyr* derives from the Latin *memoria*; one meaning of the Welsh word is 'grave'. This suggests that the chapel was built over Eilian's tomb shrine.[31]

Until the mid-nineteenth century, pilgrims came from all parts of north Wales to Eilian's well, near the shore, for a blessing on cattle and corn and for the cure of fever, fits, tuberculosis and other diseases; the well was also visited in order to curse one's enemies.[32] Pilgrims' offerings were placed in a chest inside the church. A feature of the church is its twelfth-century tower capped with a spire; a fine fifteenth-century oak rood screen separates the chancel from the nave (see photo opposite).

Seiriol of Penmon

The monastery of Penmon is at the eastern tip of Anglesey, three miles north-north-east of Beaumaris. As with many early Christian sites, the isolation of its idyllic setting is misleading, for the monastery is surrounded by four clusters of hut circles, the remains of a large Celtic village of at least 300 inhabitants. Between the groups of homes, terraces survive to show that farming was practised.[33]

St Eilian's wooden shrine in his chapel, Llaneilian, Anglesey.

Oak rood screen, Llaneilian, Anglesey.

Penmon is said to have been founded by Einion, Prince of Llŷn, one of the Sons of Cunedda; he appointed his nephew, Seiriol, as head of the community. The circular stone wall of an early cell is protected by a sheltering cliff. Beside its remains are the foundations of Seiriol's well and its antechamber, where several people could sit. The brickwork over the well is more recent: the red bricks do not blend with the solid stones that surround the pool below. The well was revered through the centuries, and the well-keeper lived in a house nearby.

The present church was built in the twelfth century to replace a wooden one burnt by Vikings in 971. Two fine tenth-century carved crosses are preserved inside the church; they show Irish and Scandinavian influence, and are thought to originate from a school of sculptors based in Cheshire.[34] From the monastery, there is a magnificent view across the Conwy Bay towards the mountains on the mainland.

Another group of monks lived on Ynys Seiriol (now Puffin Island), half a mile offshore. The monastic cemetery was also on the island, and many monks and rulers were buried here—including, it is said, Seiriol and his cousin, Maelgwyn, King of Gwynedd. The island was not always a safe haven—in 632 King Cadwallon took refuge there while King Edwin of Northumbria laid siege to the tiny island, before capturing Anglesey. Norse settlers named the island 'Priestholm' after the priests who lived there. In medieval times, Seiriol's body was brought back from Priestholm to Penmon and buried in a shrine in the church crypt, beneath the chancel. Pilgrims descended a stone staircase to visit it.

Writing in the twelfth century, Gerald of Wales informs us that Penmon was one of three Culdee monasteries in north Wales. This monastic reform movement which originated in ninth-century Ireland was described at the end of Chapter 1. If Penmon became a Culdee

St Seiriol's well and hut circle, Penmon, Anglesey.

Right: Base of tenth-century cross, adapted as a font, at Penmon, Anglesey.

Below left: Tenth-century cross, Penmon, Anglesey.

Below right: Puffin Island, viewed from Penmon, Anglesey.

community, this suggests Irish influence, and a strong commitment to religious life. The community on Priestholm must also have flourished, for in 1237 King Llewelyn the Great granted the monastery of Penmon to the prior of Priestholm.

Later in the century, Penmon became an Augustinian friary. Dominating the site today is the friars' thirteenth-century refectory, with a dormitory above and cellars below. The men ate in silence while one of them read aloud; there is a corner seat beside a window, where the reader could take advantage of the light. The friars' main source of protein was fish; their fishpond survives, fed from Seiriol's well.[35]

The Augustinians were responsible for a fine stained-glass window above Seiriol's shrine in the church. Only two fragments of the great east window remain; they depict Saints Christopher and Seiriol, and are now combined in a small window in the south transept. Seiriol is dressed as a medieval friar in brown and white robes, with a cap and a curly beard.

Cristiolus and Nidan

Two more local Anglesey saints are Nidan and Cristiolus. The church of Llangristiolus is visible from the busy main road to Holyhead; it is 8 miles west of the Menai Bridge. Cristiolus (or 'Little Christ') is first mentioned in a document dating from 1510; he was said to be a follower of Cadfan who worked among the people of central Anglesey, which was then mainly marshland. The single-chambered church of Llangristiolus is on a ridge outside the village, with a view over the low-lying fields. It contains a fine font with ring-chain decoration, in a somewhat archaic style; it perhaps dates from the twelfth century.

Carved font, Llangristiolus, Anglesey.

Similar motifs are found on one of the high crosses at Penmon and on the font at Trefdraeth, 2 miles south-west of Llangristiolus, while there is a more elaborate example in Beuno's church at Pistyll, on the Llŷn peninsula. Llangristiolus church was rebuilt in the fifteenth century; its chancel dates from the early sixteenth century. The key to the church can be obtained from the house next door.

Llanidan

Nidan was said to have been a disciple of Kentigern of Glasgow, and was associated with Penmon; he is first named in a document dating from about 1300. The ruined church at Llanidan is very large, and dates from the fourteenth and fifteenth century. An oblong stone reliquary with a gabled roof was found beneath the church in the nineteenth century; it contained fragments of bone. The shrine has been assigned a fourteenth-century date, but its simple construction suggests that it might be earlier; it perhaps contained relics of Nidan.

There was also a chapel dedicated to Beuno at Llanidan; it contained a bell known as *cloch felen Beuno*, or 'Beuno's yellow bell', describing its burnished metal, but it was lost in the eighteenth century. Llanidan is near the Anglesey shore, overlooking the Menai Strait, 4 miles south-west of Llanfair Pwyllgwyngyll. The ruined church can be reached from the A4080: 1.5 miles past the exit for Llanddaniel Fab, turn left at the first crossroads, with a lodge on the corner, and proceed down the lane to the end. To visit the church, go on a weekday, approach the locked gates of the adjacent house, and sound your car horn until a groundsman appears with the keys.

Arcade of the ruined church, Llanidan, Anglesey.

Saints of the Borderland:
Asaf, Marcella and Garmon

From the fifth century onwards and throughout medieval times, Denbighshire and the surrounding area of north Wales was disputed borderland. It was named *Y Berfeddwlad*, meaning 'the Middle Country' or 'the Lands Between'; this region lay between the Welsh principalities of Gwynedd to the west and Powys to the south, and it also lay between England and the heartland of north Wales.[1]

When the Romans withdrew in the early fifth century, the 'Middle Country' was already disputed territory claimed by rival native rulers. These Welsh warlords, recorded on Eliseg's Pillar, claimed descent from Roman Emperors and Welsh founding heroes, and sought the blessing of the Church. The Anglo-Saxons began to attack this territory; they were fought by the kings of Powys, Cyngen, and Elisedd mentioned on the pillar, but the Saxons proved too strong; eventually, the more powerful kings of Gwynedd repelled them.[2]

Eliseg's Pillar

This royal stone cross at Valle Crucis, 3 miles north of Llangollen, records and praises the achievements of the kings of Powys. It dates from between 808 and 855, and was erected by King Cyngen ap Cadell, the ruler of Powys. The cross that gave the valley its name no longer survives, but much of the lengthy inscription at its base was transcribed in 1696 by the antiquarian Edward Lhuyd before it became too weathered to decipher. The lower half of the pillar, with its text, is now lost.

The inscription was intended to be declaimed, both as a proclamation and a prayer. It honours Cyngen's great-grandfather, Elisedd ap Gwylog, and is one of the longest inscriptions to survive from pre-Viking Wales. It recalls Elisedd's military victories against the English from Mercia during the last years of the reign of King Æthelbald and the early years of King Offa's rule, and describes Elisedd's subsequent recovery of Powys in around 757.

It is possible that Cyngen regained control of Powys in a similar way, after Mercian incursions early in his reign, and that the pillar is a victory monument which juxtaposes and celebrates the military successes of generations of rulers of Powys.[3] The inscription recalls how Germanus (*c.* 378–*c.* 448), an early bishop from Gaul who preached in Britain, blessed the royal line of Powys, which was founded by the semi-legendary hero Vortigern. The self-styled emperor Magnus Maximus (*c.* 335–88) is also commemorated as a noble ancestor. The inscription reads:

+ Concenn [i.e. Cyngen] son of Cattell, Cattell son of Brochmail, Brochmail son of Eliseg [i.e. Elisedd], Eliseg son of Guoillauc.

+ And that Concenn, great-grandson of Eliseg erected this stone for his great-grandfather Eliseg.

+ It is Eliseg who joined together the inheritance of Powys throughout nine [?years] out of the power of the Angles, with his sword and fire.

+ Whosoever shall read this hand-inscribed stone, let him give a blessing on the soul of Eliseg.

+ This is that Concenn who captured with his hand 1100 acres which used to belong to his kingdom of Powys…

+ Britu was the son of Vortigern, whom Germanus [Bishop of Auxerre] blessed and whom Severa bore to him, the daughter of [Magnus] Maximus, the king of the Romans.

+ Conmarch painted this writing at the command of his king Concenn.

+ The blessing of the Lord be upon Concenn and upon his entire household, and upon the entire region of Powys until the Day of Judgement. Amen.[4]

Besides being an invitation to prayer, the pillar is also a statement of political propaganda; the cylindrical form of the pillar evokes a Roman triumphal column. The monument may have served as a place of assembly or a site of royal inauguration. It is carved in Latin half-uncial script, and so resembles a land charter.[5]

The cross was erected on a far older mound, linking the past with the present; it honours legendary ancestors, showing how ninth-century genealogies could be manipulated for political ends.[6] The mound on which the pillar stands was originally an Early Bronze Age burial cairn which had probably been long abandoned, but its ruins may still have been visible, and in the ninth century the site was evidently considered as a fitting setting for a royal cross.[7]

The Normans

After 1066, the Normans attacked Wales, led in the north by freelance adventurers called 'Marchers' or borderers, who built castles and fought with mounted knights. It seemed likely that they would overrun the entire country, but the princes of Gwynedd once again led a powerful counter-attack and forced them eastwards. Throughout the twelfth and early thirteenth centuries, Welsh rulers and Anglo-Norman Marchers struggled to control the borderland. During a period of peace, a local ruler founded Valle Crucis Abbey in 1201. In 1267, the last Prince Llywelyn of Gwynedd was confirmed by the English as Prince of Wales, but in 1283 the region was finally taken over by the English.[8]

The Borderland in Medieval Times

The borderland was divided into districts, or *cantrefi*—a word meaning 'a hundred settlements'. They still retain their local character today, and often mark the boundary between dialects. Some were originally kingdoms, while others may have been created later. Each *cantref* had its own court, which was an assembly of the main landowners of the *cantref*; the court was presided over by the king, or his representative.

In the north were the so-called 'Four *Cantrefi*'. One was Rhos, between the rivers Elwy and Conwy; St Asaph's cathedral was on the Elwy. Another was Tegeingl, or Flintshire, on the coast between Rhuddlan and the Dee estuary; its religious centre was Winifred's well at Holywell. The third northern *cantref* was Rhufoniog in the uplands, consisting of western Denbighshire, with its capital at Denbigh, whose mother church was named after Marcella. The fourth *cantref* was the fertile, southern Vale of Clwyd, centred upon Ruthin; its mother church was dedicated to Mawgan.

To the east lay the hilly *cantref* of Iâl, or Yale, which would much later give its name to the American university; its chief monastery was dedicated to Garmon. There were also other monasteries, each named after local saints, in this comparatively well-populated region of Wales.

Mawgan

Llanrhudd, or 'red church' is so-named because it is partly built of local red sandstone. The church is dedicated to Mawgan, or Meugan, and is a mile east of Ruthin, or 'red fort', built on a ridge above the River Clwyd. The church contains a fine carved rood screen separating the nave from the chancel. In the churchyard, near the south porch, is a decorated shaft of a medieval preaching cross, 3 metres tall (see photo opposite).

Mawgan was a Welsh monk who was possibly a hermit from Caerleon in south Wales; he is commemorated in a number of places, particularly in the Teifi valley in Ceredigion, but no medieval Life of him survives. In Rhygyfarch's eleventh-century *Life of David*, when his father, King Sant of Ceredigion, finds a stag, a fish and a swarm of bees, which indicate the property rights of his future son, he is told by an angel to take the honeycomb and a portion of the fish and the stag to the 'monastery of Maucannus' (or Mawgan in Welsh). Rhygyfarch adds: 'To this day it is called the Monastery of the Deposit'.[9] It is not known where this monastery was, or indeed, whether it existed.

There were two early Cornish monasteries dedicated to a monk named Mawgan—one was at St Mawgan-in-Meneage on the Lizard peninsula. 'Meneage' means 'land of the monks', and there is an inscribed grave marker dating from AD 600 in the village. Another early site is St Mawgan-in-Pydar, 4 miles north-east of Newquay, where there is a fine tenth-century cross that was carved by a sculptor named Runhol.

Mawgan, or Meugan, was a common name in early medieval times. St Mawgan might possibly be identified with a poet named Mawgan, writing in the seventh or eighth century, whose metrical Latin prayers, *Orationes Moucani*, survive in an eighth-century manuscript from Worcester.[10] Their dominant theme is an urgent plea to God for salvation by the sinful poet.

Cross shaft at St Mawgan's church, Llanrhudd, Denbighshire.

Tudno

This monk gave his name to Llandudno, in the *cantref* of Rhos. A church is dedicated to Tudno on the headland of the Great Orme, above the modern town of Llandudno. 'Orme' is Old Norse for 'great worm', or sea-serpent; it was perhaps named by the Vikings because of the shape of the headland. The Great Orme was well known in early times: copper was mined here from the Bronze Age until the nineteenth century.

According to legend, Tudno was one of the seven sons of Seithenyn, who ruled over territory which was submerged in Cardigan Bay. The brothers are supposed to have then sought refuge in the monastery of Bangor Is-coed, where Tudno became a monk, before travelling to the headland of the Great Orme, where *Ogof Lech*, a small limestone cave containing a freshwater spring, is associated with Tudno. One of the thirteen treasures of Britain was said to be Tudno's whetstone, which sharpened the sword of a hero but blunted that of a coward.

A stone church was built here in the twelfth century; the carved bowl of its font still survives. In medieval times, Llandudno was a cluster of farms around Tudno's church, and it remained a small community until a holiday resort grew along the strand below in the nineteenth century. A flock of feral goats has been reintroduced onto the Great Orme; they roamed wild in early times, and feature in the Lives of monks. However, the goats that one sees there today are from Kashmir; they have been on the Orme since the 1890s.

The key to the church is held at the farm below the churchyard. There is a holy well near the church; to find it, walk up the road past the church and take the second footpath to the left towards Pink Farm, signed 'Ski Llandudno'. The well is on the right, 100 metres along the track, just inside a field.

Feral goats at Llandudno, Conwy.

St Asaph

At a time when waterways were as important as roads, St Asaph was in a key position at the junction of the rivers Elwy and Clwyd. St Asaph is near the north Welsh coast, 5 miles south of Rhyl, and was therefore also easily accessible from the sea. The present cathedral dates mainly from the thirteenth century; it is set on the hillside above the river valley.

Its Welsh name, Llanelwy, refers not to a saint, but to the nearby river. In this it resembles Llandaf, which is at the lowest crossing point of the River Taf. Both cathedrals lacked a founding saint, and therefore attempted to acquire one. St Asaph became a cathedral town quite late: in 1125 it was not named, but was simply referred to as the diocese between those of Chester and Bangor. The Anglo-Norman diocesan church of Llanelwy was established in 1143 under Bishop Gilbert. It acquired its dedication to Asaf even later: the name is first recorded in 1152, when Geoffrey of Monmouth succeeded Gilbert as bishop.[11]

Asaf appears to have been a local saint whose cult originated at Llanasa, which will be described below. Perhaps he was not considered sufficiently important to be attributed the honour of being the cathedral's founding saint, or perhaps it was common knowledge that Asaf had never been associated with the cathedral. For whatever reason, a 'foundation story' was created, and Kentigern, an early bishop of Strathclyde, was described as establishing the cathedral.

It is unclear why Kentigern was chosen as St Asaph's founding saint. The tradition may have been devised in about 1125, when the diocese of York was trying to acquire St Asaph and also attempting to establish its authority over Scottish territory, although

St Asaph's cathedral, Denbighshire.

both ventures were unsuccessful. Perhaps it was considered that Jocelin, a skilful biographer from a Yorkshire monastery, could create a noble Life of Kentigern that would link the diocese of Glasgow with that of St Asaph. The story could plausibly be situated within the migration of political exiles from Strathclyde to north Wales.

Jocelin's *Life of Kentigern*

A Briton who became bishop of Glasgow in the early seventh century, Kentigern's name means 'Chief Prince'. We know little about him, but we do know that he existed, since his name appears in early texts. Jocelin (fl. 1175–1214) was a Cistercian monk of Furness Abbey in Cumbria. The *Life of Kentigern* was commissioned by his namesake and fellow Cistercian Jocelin, Bishop of Glasgow; it was intended to replace an earlier Life of Kentigern written at the request of Herbert, Bishop of Glasgow, of which only a fragment survives.

   Although Jocelin's Life is largely based on legend, it may contain a few facts. He relates that when an anti-Christian chieftain came to power, Kentigern fled south—first to Cumbria and then to Wales. Jocelin describes Kentigern arriving at Carlisle and proceeding to Crosthwaite. This and a number of other churches in Cumbria are dedicated to Kentigern, some using his pet-name, Mungo, meaning 'My Dear One'. The Cumbrian dedications may reflect the recovery of this region by the kingdom of Strathclyde in the tenth century.

   Jocelin recounts how Kentigern established a monastery at St Asaph, travelling by a circuitous route. Kentigern arrives in south-west Wales and first visits St David's; this affords an opportunity for David, the chief saint of Wales, to acclaim the holiness and authority of Kentigern.[12] Next, King Cadwallon invites Kentigern to build a monastery at Llancarfan, although this is to become Cadog's chief cult centre; Kentigern is, however, connected by Jocelin with this important site.[13]

Kentigern Founds a Monastery

A wild white boar shows Kentigern where he should build his church, a feature also found in the story of Cadog and of other Celtic saints.[14, 15] Maelgwyn Gwynedd now arrives on the scene and says the land belongs to him. In a story that echoes the conversion of St Paul in the New Testament (Acts 9. 1–19), Maelgwyn destroys the monastery and is struck blind; Kentigern heals him and baptises him. In gratitude, King Maelgwyn asks him to found a monastery in Powys, on land beside the River Elwy:

> [Kentigern] laid his healing hand on the blinded man in the name of the Lord, and signing him with the cross of salvation, turned his night into day. No sooner therefore was he restored to sight than he was dipped by the holy bishop in the saving water [of baptism], and henceforward he became an active and devoted fellow-worker…
>
> Taking an account of all his possessions, he bestowed them all on St Kentigern for the construction of his monastery, and, aided by this assistance, [Kentigern] rapidly brought what he had commenced to perfection. He established the Cathedral Chair of his bishopric, the diocese of which was the greater portion of the surrounding country, which he had acquired for the Lord by his preaching.[16]

The *Red Book of St Asaf*, a manuscript dating from the thirteenth or fourteenth century, is known to have contained a Life of Asaf. It is now lost, but a text dating from 1256, attached to the *Red Book* and appartenly independent of Jocelin's *Life of Kentigern*, also relates that Maelgwyn Gwynedd was involved with Kentigern in establishing a monastery at St Asaph, although under different circumstances.[17]

Kentigern's Disciple, Asaf

Asaf now enters the story: Jocelin describes how he was Kentigern's finest disciple. He is of noble birth, a grandson of Pabo Post Pryden, and virtuous—and therefore suitable for the monastery to be entrusted to his care:

> There was one among [the monks], Asaf by name and famous by descent and appearance, who shone in virtues and wonders from the flower of his earliest puberty. He was diligent to follow the life and teaching of his master [Kentigern], as it is possible to know completely from reading his life that was transcribed into a little book.[18]

The 'little book' (*libellum* in Latin), was another Life of Asaf, now lost. Jocelin attributes a miracle to young Asaf. Abbot Kentigern had been chanting the psalms in the winter, standing in the river; he came out and dressed, but developed hypothermia. He asked Asaf to fetch live coals from the oven to warm himself and Asaf did so, carrying them in the folds of his clothes, which remained undamaged. Each of the two monks attributes the miracle to the sanctity of the other; both are therefore equals in power and holiness.[19]

Kentigern ordains Asaf, and designates him as his successor:

St Kentigern who up till then had held dear and beloved the venerable boy Asaf, from that day forward prized him as the most dear and most special of all. And as soon as he was duly able, he advanced him to holy orders. And in due time he entrusted the care of the monastery to him, and made him his successor in the bishopric.[20]

According to Jocelin, Kentigern left Wales and returned to Strathclyde at the request of its ruler—Rhydderch Hael, or Roderick 'the Generous'. If this were so, it gives us an early seventh-century date for Kentigern, since Rhydderch is described as a contemporary of Columba (d. 597) in the Life of Columba written by Adomnán, the ninth abbot of Iona, in about 697. Rhydderch may have asked Kentigern to become bishop of Glasgow; alternatively, Glasgow may have become a bishopric only in the twelfth century.[21]

Jocelin describes how Kentigern took many monks back to Strathclyde, but a third of the community remained with Asaf:

[Kentigern] enthroned St Asaf on the cathedral seat…. A very large portion of the brothers, numbering 665, went with Kentigern as they were in no way able or willing to live without him, as long as he lived. Only 300 stayed behind with St Asaf.[22]

It is interesting that the brothers are depicted as being free to choose whether to stay with Asaf or leave with Kentigern.

The rest of Jocelin's Life concerns Kentigern's activity in Glasgow. The description of his last days offers the strongest evidence that Jocelin based some of his narrative on an early source, which he quotes without understanding its meaning. Jocelin relates that the elderly bishop Kentigern died after taking a warm bath on the feast of the Epiphany. In fact, in the seventh century, Celtic Christians were baptised on this feast, as they still are in Orthodox Churches, although this custom died out in Britain soon after Kentigern's lifetime.

In Jocelin's narrative, Kentigern collapsed while he was baptising candidates, in his role as bishop, at the cathedral on the feast of the Epiphany. After preaching, he was assisted to the large baptismal font. The water was warmed and Kentigern began to immerse the candidates, but the effort was too great; he collapsed and died a week later.[23]

And when the eighth day dawned from the Sunday of Epiphany, in which day the kind bishop was accustomed to wash a multitude of people in the sacred waters of baptism, it was a day surely desired by Kentigern and by the spirits of his adopted sons. Being carried by their hands, the saint entered into a small bath filled with hot water after having first sanctified it by the sign of salvation, and a crown of brothers surrounded him and waited the end of the affair. And when the saint had embraced a little rest in [the bath], he raised his hands and his eyes to heaven, bowed his head, and surrendered his spirit…. The disciples, seeing what had happened, raised his holy body up from that bath.[24]

Llanasa

The church at Llanasa is dedicated to Saints Asaf and Cyndeyrn. Cyndeyrn is Welsh for Kentigern, so this church is named after the bishop of Glasgow and his disciple, Asaf. The dedication is likely to be later than the name of the settlement, for Llanasa means 'church of Asaf', and this appears to have been his original foundation.

Celtic monks liked to choose names of Old Testament characters, and Asaph was the name of King David's cantor, according to the Books of Chronicles (1 Chron. 6. 39; 2 Chron. 5. 12). David was believed to be the author of the 150 psalms, but twelve of the psalms are also ascribed to Asaph. Monks spent much of their time chanting psalms in church, and so David and Asaf were considered appropriate monastic names. Since Asaph was a cantor in the ancient Jewish temple, according to the Old Testament, this suggests that the Welsh monk was given his name on account of his strong singing voice.

The village of Llanasa is in a sheltered valley near the north Welsh coast, 6 miles north-east of St Asaph. The church is recorded in Domesday Book (1086); since this was compiled in late Saxon times, the church must pre-date Norman settlement of the area. The present double-chambered church was constructed in the fifteenth century; it has an asymmetrical bell turret that houses two bells (see photo opposite).

In 1540, when the monasteries were dissolved at the Reformation, two fine stained-glass windows were brought to Llanasa church from Basingwerk Abbey, in Holywell. The window over the altar depicts four saints—including Beuno, dressed as a bishop. To his right, Winifred is present with a scar around her throat, although she is named (probably incorrectly) as St Catherine.[25] The church also contains the fourteenth-century tombstone of the father of Owain Glyndŵr, the last Welsh fighting prince who rose against the English and died in 1416.

Eurgain

While Winifred is the most famous female saint of north Powys, two women with a more local cult are Eurgain and Marcella. Llaneurgain (or Northop in English) is 6 miles south-east of Winifred's shrine at Holywell, and 3 miles south of the Dee estuary. Eurgain was said to be one of Cunedda's descendants, a daughter of the sixth-century king, Maelgwyn Gwynedd. Her name derives from *eur* ('gold') and *cain* ('beautiful'), and is intended to describe her character.

According to local legend, Eurgain lived on land given her by Maelgwyn at Cilcain (or 'cell of the Beautiful One'), 5 miles south-west of Llaneurgain.[26] Cilcain is an isolated

Bell turret, Llanasa church, Flintshire.

village in a valley named *Nant Gain*, or 'valley of the Beautiful One', with a stream flowing to the south. Eurgain is also associated with *Cefn Eurgain*, (Eurgain's ridge) where one can find *Tŷ Eurgain* (Eurgain's house) and *Bryn Eurgain* (Eurgain's hill).[27]

Eurgain was said to be the wife of Elidyr Mwyn-fawr 'The Courteous', one of the Men of the North who invaded Gwynedd; he was slain near Caernarfon. Eurgain is celebrated as a wife and mother, rather than as a single vowed woman. There is a tradition that she was buried beneath a mound in the hamlet of Criccin, a mile outside Rhuddlan.

Eurgain's splendid late medieval church dominates the small town of Llaneurgain (see photo overleaf). Her festival, 29 June (also the feast of Ss Peter and Paul), appears in fifteenth-century Welsh calendars; in the late medieval period, St Peter therefore became an additional patron of Llaneurgain church. A stone church was built here in the twelfth century; its fine tower was completed in 1577. The church was extensively rebuilt in the nineteenth century. The town's sixteenth-century grammar school still stands inside the churchyard, against its east wall. There was also a chapel dedicated to Eurgain in Llangian parish, near the southern tip of the Llŷn peninsula.[28]

Marcella and her Brothers

The church of Marcella (or Marchell, in Welsh) at Whitchurch is 1.5 miles east of the old walled town that was formerly at the centre of Denbigh; it is the mother church of Denbigh, and is still regarded as its parish church. It is also the most imposing of the medieval churches of Denbighshire (see photo on p. 151). Marcella is said to have been a

St Eurgain's church, Llaneurgain, Flintshire.

nun who established a hermitage here, beside a holy well. Another church is dedicated to Marcella at Marchwiel, 15 miles south-east of Whitchurch. It was rebuilt in the eighteenth century; the churchyard contains a number of old yew trees.

In local legend, different saints with nearby dedications were often said to be related to each other, and Marcella was considered to be the sister of Deifor, after whom Bodfari (see colour plate 14) is named; Bodfari is 5 miles north-east of Whitchurch, and was associated with Winifred's journey from Holywell to Gwytherin, as we saw in Chapter 7. Marcella was also said to be Tyrnog's sister; he gave his name to the church of Llanddyrnog, 3 miles east of Whitchurch.

Llanddyrnog church mainly dates from the fifteenth century; a magnificent stained-glass east window was created in about 1490. It is a 'Sacrament window'—one of nine in Britain, and the only Welsh example. The sacraments issue from the wounds of Christ on the cross, to which they are connected by red streams of blood, flowing from his hands, side and feet.

The panels above the seven sacraments depict local saints: in the uppermost panels, Asaf and Deiniol are portrayed as bishops, while below them is a row of female saints— Marcella and Winifred, Our Lady with the angel Gabriel, Frideswide of Oxford, and Catherine of Alexandria, depicted with the wheel on which she was martyred. Inside the church there is also a fine medieval dug-out oak chest for offerings.

St Marcella's church, Whitchurch, Denbighshire.

Garmon

Garmon was a native saint of Powys; a scattering of churches and wells are dedicated to him in Denbighshire, Montgomery, Radnor and Flintshire. The large churchyard of Llanarmon-yn-Iâl (or 'church of Garmon in the hills') is likely to be the site of his monastery; it was the home of a *clas* community, where clergy lived and worshipped together. It is on a hilltop site above the River Alun, 5 miles south-east of Ruthin, and was the capital of the upland region of Iâl.

The present church dates from the thirteenth century. Pilgrims came to Garmon's shrine until the Reformation; their offerings would have helped to finance the building of the double nave, which was considered necessary to accommodate the crowds who flocked to the shrine. The Tudor antiquarian John Leland describes an annual pilgrimage to Llanarmon-yn-Iâl, when offerings were made in the presence of a statue of Garmon dressed in priestly vestments.

There is a recumbent effigy of a medieval monk named Cyrus in the church, which also possesses a beautiful brass candelabra dating from 1450, depicting the Virgin and Child (the babe is now missing) enfolded by vine leaves; this may have come from Valle Crucis Abbey, whose monks owned the church. It was extensively restored in the 1730s, giving it a Georgian character that is unusual in this region.

St German's Cathedral

St German's cathedral at Peel, on the Isle of Man, halfway along its west coast, may also be named after Garmon; it occupies the crest of St Patrick's Isle. Until the eighteenth century this was a tidal islet, accessible on foot at low tide. There is now a causeway leading to the island, which is dominated by the medieval cathedral and a later castle. The island was inhabited from early times, and a number of round houses dating from around 400 BC have been excavated.

Later, there was a Christian community on St Patrick's Isle; from the seventh century onwards there was an extensive cemetery at the southern end of the island, near the medieval cathedral. Lintel graves and fragments of crosses dating from the seventh and eighth centuries were found beneath the south transept of the cathedral.[29]

The ruins of a church, a chapel and a round tower survive from the monastery, each dating in part from the tenth century. St Patrick's church was constructed of roughly dressed local red sandstone. It had *antae* (or side walls) projecting beyond the line of the gables; this style of building was common in Ireland. St Patrick's chapel (see colour plate 20) is smaller, but of similar construction.

An early altar slab was found when the two churches were restored in 1873. It is decorated with five small crosses set within a larger one; it perhaps formed the front panel of a stone altar. Near St Patrick's church is the squat, 15-metre-high round tower. Four windows facing the compass points near the top indicate that this was its original height. It, too, is built of red sandstone; its battlemented parapet was added in about 1600.[30]

The monastery was ravaged by Viking raiders, and the little island became a base for Norse settlers. They built the fort of timber, or 'pile', which gave Peel its name. Excavations have produced evidence of at least seven pagan burials within the Christian cemetery. The richest grave was that of a Viking woman who was interred with her cooking spit; this was a symbol of domestic power in Scandinavia.

At her side were her knives and sewing equipment, including a workbox, needle, and shears. She wore a magnificent necklace of seventy-three glass, amber and jet beads—some already centuries old.[31] The burial of a wealthy pagan Norsewoman in a Christian cemetery reflects the mixture of material cultures and beliefs on the island. Manx Vikings were among those who invaded Wales and settled, briefly, on Anglesey.

St Dyfnog's Pool

Dyfnog was a local monk to whom the church at Llanrhaeadr-yng-Nghinmeirch is dedicated. The village is 3 miles south-east of Denbigh; its name means 'church of the waterfall in the district of Cinmeirch'. *Rhaeadr*, or 'cascade', describes the water that gushes from the hillside into Dyfnog's pool in the woodland above the church. This was a healing well visited by many pilgrims, and so the church was endowed generously.

Beyond the churchyard is a range of Georgian almshouses, still in use. A path in front of them leads under an archway into a wood. Dyfnog's well can be found by turning right and following the path upwards, along the stream. Soon, a large stone-edged pool, paved with marble, is visible ahead, fed by streams from the rock face. A medieval Welsh poet wrote that he 'reveres Dyfnog's effigy, accepts his miracles, praises his wonder-working well, which gives grace to all nations … indeed there was none like it'.[32]

In the 1690s the antiquarian Edward Lhuyd described how the pool was once covered by a roofed building where pilgrims bathed, hoping to be cured of skin diseases, 'scabs and the itch, and some said it cured [small]pox'.[33] Browne Willis wrote in the eighteenth century that it was 'provided with all conveniences of rooms etc for bathing built about it'.[34] According to Richard Fenton, in the early nineteenth century the well was:

> …arched over, from which the water used to fall through a pipe in the wall into a bath, whose bottom was paved with marble, with a building round it and roofed, but now exhibiting one shapeless ruin.[35]

Writing in 1883, Thomas Pennant added:

> The fountain was enclosed in an angular well, decorated with small human figures, and before the well [a pool] for the use of pious bathers.[36, 37]

Dyfnog's church was enriched with gifts from pilgrims visiting the well; a very large dug-out chest for offerings survives. The chancel has a fine, fifteenth-century, barrel-vaulted roof, with carved vines and angels holding the instruments of Christ's passion. The porch is decorated with carved oak taken from the former rood screen, and is surmounted by a niche that would have contained a statue of Dyfnog until it was destroyed at the Reformation.

St Dyfnog's pool, Llanrhaeadr-yng-Nghinmeirch, Denbighshire.

The Jesse window in St Dyfnog's church, Llanrhaeadr-yng-Nghinmeirch, Denbighshire.

There is a magnificent Jesse window dating from 1533; it is one of the finest in Britain. The window depicts the family tree of Christ; the tree springs from the loins of Jesse, the father of King David, using an image taken from the prophet Isaiah: 'A shoot shall spring from the stock of Jesse' (Isiah 11. 1). In the centre, King David plays the harp while, near the top, the Virgin and Child stand surrounded by the sun's rays. In the Civil War of 1642, the Jesse window was removed, placed in the dug-out chest and buried; it was replaced at the Restoration of the Monarchy in 1661.

Betws Gwerfil Goch

Four miles north-west of Corwen, the remote hamlet of Betws Gwerfil Goch, or 'Prayer-house of Gwerfil the Red[-head]' lies in a steep-sided valley on an ancient pilgrims' trackway across Wales. The prayer house was established for pilgrims in the twelfth century by the red-haired Princess Gwerfil of Meirionydd; she was the granddaughter of King Owain Gwynedd of north Wales. Her father, Lord Cynan of Meirionnydd, died in 1174. The Ode to Cadfan (see Chapter 6) was probably composed to be sung in his presence.

Princess Gwerfil's church was rebuilt in the fifteenth century. Behind the altar are unique wooden panels, which once formed part of the rood screen that separated the chancel from the nave. They were carved locally, in an unsophisticated style, in the late fifteenth century, and survived destruction at the Reformation only because of the hamlet's remoteness. The central panel depicts a cloaked Christ beneath the Latin words spoken by Pontius Pilate, '*Ecce homo*', or 'Behold the man' (John 19. 5). On either side are the weeping figures of Our Lady and John the Evangelist, flanked by symbols of Christ's passion—a hammer, a spear, a club, pincers, nails and a crown of thorns.

Most churches with the name-element *betws* are dependant chapels, which were perhaps established by individuals who created their own private churches within an already-developing parish system. Other examples of *betws* place-names that probably include their founder's names are Betws Bledrws and Betws Leucu in Ceredigion, and Betws Cedewain in Monmouthshire.[38]

The word *betws* is borrowed from Old English *bed-hus*, an oratory where people 'told their beads', or prayed the rosary. Betws first occurs as a place-name element at the start of the thirteenth century and is not recorded as a noun until the fifteenth century. There seem to be no examples of this place-name element in England.[39]

Saints of Llŷn and Bardsey; Hermit Life

It has been suggested that the Llŷn peninsula may derive its name from the Irish word *Laigin*, meaning 'people of Leinster'.[1] While people from northern Ireland migrated to Galloway in southern Scotland, a distance of 20 miles by sea, others from south-east Ireland made the 30-mile journey to the Llŷn peninsula.

We have already examined a number of sites on the Llŷn peninsula. Beuno's monastery at Clynnog Fawr was discussed in Chapter 7, together with other sites associated with his cult at Pistyll and Llanaelhaearn. Cybi's holy well at Llangybi was described in Chapter 8. In this chapter, we will focus on Bardsey Island and the early settlements at the western end of the peninsula.

Llangwynnadl

The Llŷn peninsula must have resembled a busy summer holiday resort in late medieval times, as hundreds of pilgrims walked along the peninsula to Aberdaron, at its western end, in order to take the boat to Bardsey Island (see colour plate 22). Llangwynnadl became one of the main stopping places on the 'Saints' Way', since it is only 5 miles north-east of Aberdaron. Llangwynnadl is named after a sixth-century monk named Vendesetl, or, in its later form, Gwynhoedl—meaning 'One of pure, or bright, life'.

Vendesetl's sixth-century tombstone can be seen at Llanbedrog, 4 miles south-west of Pwllheli. The name VENDESETLI is carved on a tall, slender column of black basalt brought from Llannor, which is only 4 miles north-east of Llanbedrog. The tombstone can be seen, together with another sixth-century basalt pillar commemorating Iuvenalis, the son of Edern, in the porch of the Gallery and Arts Centre, to the left of Llanbedrog church. The name Edern derives from the Latin 'Eternus', and means '[Possessing] eternal [life]'. Edern gave his name to a neighbouring settlement.

In later medieval times, the people of Llangwynnadl were keen to claim that their patron saint was buried among them, instead of somewhere else, and a Latin inscription, carved around a pillar in the nave of the church in about 1520, reads: 'S. Gwynhoedl iacet hic', or 'Saint Gwynhoedl lies here'.

At the same time, a second and third nave were added to the church to accommodate the crowds of pilgrims. A fine new font was also carved, featuring the heads of King Henry

VIII and Bishop Skeffington of Bangor. Across the small river that flows past the church to the sea, a large field was named *Cae Eisteddfa*, or Hospice Field. Pilgrims could camp here before continuing their journey to or from Bardsey Island.

A Monk's Handbell

An early handbell survives from Llangwynnadl; it is of cast bronze and is 17 cm high. Unusually, the bell is decorated with an animal head at each end of its handle. It is now in the National Museum of Wales, in Cardiff. Eight early medieval bells survive from Wales and the Marches: three from Caernarfon (Llanarmon, Llangwynnadl, and Llangystennin), and one each from Anglesey (Llanrhyddlad), Conwy (Dolwyddelan), Brecon (Llangenny), and Herefordshire (Marden). All are roughly rectangular, with a handle at the top.[2]

They range in size from about 4–12 inches high; the larger ones are made from folded sheet iron, coated in bronze and riveted together, while the smaller ones are of cast bronze. Irish parallels suggest that the iron bells were manufactured from at least AD 600, while the cast bronze bells, like that at Llangwynnadl, date from around 700–900. Their size and the shape of their handles suggest that all of them were portable handbells.[3]

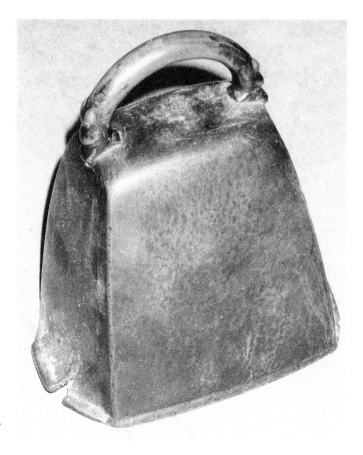

Replica of early handbell, Llangwynnadl, Gwynedd.

Aberdaron

Close to the tip of the Llŷn peninsula, Aberdaron church is dedicated to two of Cadfan's followers—Hywyn and Lleuddad. The lower part of the church has been buried by drifting sand. It has a Norman porch, and by the twelfth century it had a sanctuary seat—a stone chair in which those taking refuge from the law could claim immunity before sailing to safety in another land.

This was a *clas* church—a monastery without a rule, whose headship was hereditary. The Normans destroyed the *clas* system since they preferred to control churches in their territory, but because of its remotenesss, Aberdaron remained a *clas* church until the Reformation. In the fifteenth century, the church was doubled in size to accommodate pilgrims. A hospice where they slept is known as 'The Great Kitchen' (*Y Gegin Fawr*); the present building dates from about 1300 (see photo opposite). Here, travellers could rest in comfort before their rough sea journey to Bardsey Island.

There were two embarkation points near Aberdaron. One of these was at Brach-y-Pwyll, where the foundations of a chapel are visible in the turf above the shore. Down among the rocks is *Ffynnon Fair* ('St Mary's Well'), a freshwater spring visible at low tide. Here, travellers could fill their water bottles before they embarked.

A Monastery at Capel Anelog

It is not known whether a monastery was continuously occupied on Bardsey in early times; it may have been used only as a Lenten retreat by monks living on the mainland at Aberdaron, or at the monastery of Capel Anelog, 2 miles north-west of Aberdaron. Two gravestones were found at Capel Anelog, dating from the late fifth or early sixth century. One of them reads: 'SENACVS PR[E]SB[YTER] HIC IACIT CVM MVLTITVD[I]NEM FRATRVM', or 'Senacus, priest, lies here with a great number of brothers'. The other is inscribed: 'VERACIUS P[RES]B[YTE]R HIC IACIT', or 'Veracius, priest, lies here'.[4]

This suggests that there was a monastic cemetery, and presumably a community of many brothers at Capel Anelog; the gravestones can be seen in Aberdaron church. Most early inscribed stones dating from the fifth and sixth centuries record kinship; very few mention an individual's status within the Church. Exceptionally, these two stones record that these men were priests.[5]

Lleuddad

The twelfth-century poem in praise of Cadfan coupled his name with that of Lleuddad as one of the founding saints of the monastery on Bardsey Island, as we saw in Chapter 6. Lleuddad's sixteenth-century Life elaborates on this, and claims that Lleuddad was Cadfan's successor as abbot of Bardsey. A field on the island is known as 'Lleuddad's Garden'; on the mainland, a cave at Aberdaron is named after him in addition to a well in

The Great Kitchen, Aberdaron, Gwynedd.

St Lleuddad's well, Bryncroes, Gwynedd.

Bryncroes parish, 4 miles east of Aberdaron (see photo on previous page). Its water was renowned for curing sick people and animals.

Lleuddad was a popular local saint. A late medieval Welsh prayer to Lleudadd, or Llawddog, praises him for the help he gives to those who till the soil. Part of it reads:

> The land, its trees, and its seed-corn,
> may Llawddog make all succeed.
> May Llawddog grant success
> to his people, his men and his children,
> on every harrow and every yoke,
> and on the ploughs of the lands,
> on every furrow and every hill,
> on every ridge and every seed.
> Llawddog is a single key of cultivation,
> he is a key to all the earth;
> Llawddog, I was better from praising him;
> wherever we all go, [he] is the key to heaven.[6]

Bardsey Island

The Welsh name for Bardsey is *Ynys Enlli*, or 'Island in the Current'. It lies only two miles offshore, but because of the strong currents in the Sound, the sea journey can be as much as six miles. Bardsey was inhabited from ancient times. There was a Neolithic flint factory at the northern end of the island, where a stream enters the sea: a Neolithic hammer and some 5,000 flints have been found here.

Further south, Bronze Age cremation burials have been detected close to the sandy beach that forms the present-day landing stage, where the island reaches its narrowest point. Some 300 metres to the north is a barrow, perhaps also dating from the Bronze Age, close to the sea on the opposite shore. There are two caves on the east and west slopes of Mynydd Enlli, or Enlli Mountain, at the island's north-eastern end, and today there are thirteen wells and springs in the flat land below the mountain.[7]

Seals bask on the rocks at low tide to digest their food; these would have been a valuable source of meat and blubber for early inhabitants. Blubber can be used as wax for candles and oil for lamps. A source of protein was seabirds' eggs, of which there is a plentiful supply; today, for example, there are 10,000–16,000 breeding pairs of Manx Shearwaters nesting in rabbit burrows.[8]

In early Christian times, the landing place was at the northern end of the island, at the inlet closest to the ruined Augustinian monastery (see colour plate 23). To the west of the abbey, which dates from the thirteenth century, is the field known as Lleuddad's Garden, where early herbs such as black horehound still grow. Several types of herb grow around the houses on the island, perhaps descendants of those planted by the monks.[9]

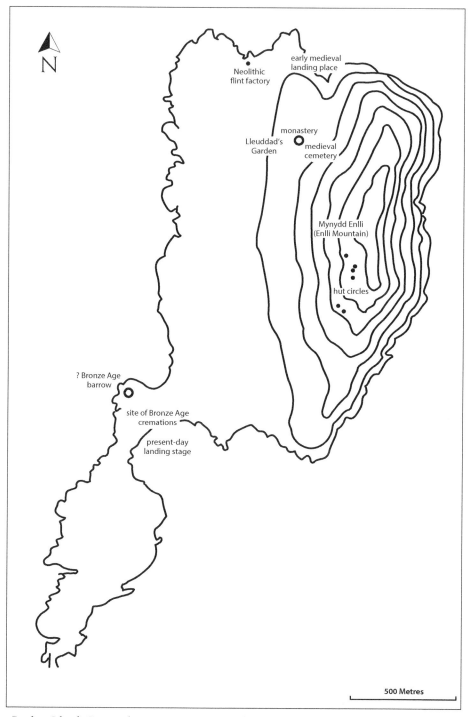

Bardsey Island. Contour lines are at 25-m intervals.

Early Graves

It is not known how soon there was a monastic presence on the island. In 2005, circular structures (suggesting monks' huts) were detected near the ruined tower of the later Augustinian abbey with the aid of a magnetometer.[10] Excavation has demonstrated the existence of an extensive cemetery around the abbey, some of which is early medieval. The graves examined so far are a mixture of cist (or slab-lined) graves, some with lintels, and simple dug graves.[11]

When the road and the island houses were rebuilt in 1873–6, burials were found with the feet pointing east. Cist burials can still be seen protruding above the surface of the unmade road beside *Tŷ Newydd*, a cottage just south of the abbey churchyard; during excavation here in 1993–8, an Anglo-Saxon penny of King Eadgar (*c.* 973) was found in one of the graves. This would suggest an early monastery here, surrounded by a cemetery.

There are also foundations of six circular huts on the western slope of Mynydd Enlli (see colour plate 24); these resemble the hut circle at Penmon on Anglesey, and could have been built by early monks, but they might be pre-Christian.[12] Bardsey is a Norse name meaning 'Bardr's Island'; in the tenth century, it may have become the base of a Viking pirate chief. The monks would then have fled, or been killed or kidnapped. If so, the monks returned, for the lower half of a cross dating from the late tenth or early eleventh century depicts a monk wearing a pleated robe that almost reaches his ankles.[13]

Bardsey in the Twelfth Century

The earliest reference to the monastery on Bardsey is a record in the twelfth-century *Chronicle of the Princes* of the death of Iardurr, a 'monk of Enlli', in 1012. A poem survives by Meilyr (d. *c.* 1137), who was the chief poet at the court of Gruffudd ap Cynan at Aberffraw. Meilyr says that he wishes to retire to Bardsey, the monastery against which the ocean beaks, in order to await his death and resurrection 'among the pure ones'—the monks on the island. He writes:

> I, Meilyr the poet, am a pilgrim to St Peter,
> the gate-warden [of heaven] who weighs the quality of worth.
> For that time when the Awakening shall come
> of us who are entombed, prepare thou me.
> May I be in the dwelling place, awaiting the call,
> of the monastery against which the ocean breaks;
> and which is a wilderness of unperishing glory,
> whose graveyard is surrounded by the breast of the sea …
> He, the Creator who formed me, will enfold me
> among the pure ones, the folk of Enlli.[14]

When Meilyr described 'the pure ones', he may be referring to the exceptional austerity of the *Céli Dé*, or Culdees on Bardsey. Writing in the twelfth century, Gerald of Wales tells us of three reformed monasteries in north Wales: on Bardsey Island, at Penmon (on Anglesey), and in Beddgelert (at the foot of Mount Snowdon). In his *Journey through Wales* (1188), Gerald described the '*coelibes* [celibates] of Ynys Enlli who were also called *colidei* [*Céli Dé*]'.[15] He added that many holy men were said to be buried on the island.

Almost thirty years later, in his *Speculum Ecclesiae* (*c.* 1220), Gerald of Wales describes the community at Beddgelert, and tells us more about the lifestyle of *Céli Dé* monks, noting their austerity:

> In Gwynedd ... there was a religious house of clerics at the foot of the mountain of Eryri, commonly called the Mountain of Snows [Snowdon] ... Here there were clerics devoted to the service of God and living in a holy manner and in common, after the example of the Apostles. They were not bound to any order of monks or canons but were celibates or Culdees, who served God and were given to abstinence, [and] continence and renowned for their charity and hospitality.[16]

In the early 1200s, the ruler of Gwynedd, Lleywelyn ap Iorweth (d. 1240) endowed a house of Augustinian canons on Bardsey, granting them a number of estates on the mainland. Until this point, Bardsey had been the home of a remote eremitical community; it now became a leading church whose superior was named in court documents, and Bardsey became a famous centre for pilgrimage.[17] The steward of the thirteenth-century community was given the title *Oeconomus*, an early Greek word originating with the desert monks of the Near East. This archaic title may have been used in earlier times by monks on Bardsey.[18]

Elgar The Hermit

In the eleventh century, before the arrival of the Augustinians, a man named Elgar came to live on the island; Elgar is an Anglo-Saxon name which probably means 'Elf-spear'. There are other signs of an English presence on Bardsey, including the Anglo-Saxon penny of King Eadgar, mentioned above, and an inscribed stone dating from some time after 750, which can now be seen in the chapel. It reads 'JESILLIMARIGUELIO', the second half of which may be Old English for 'famous Welshman' (*Merewalh*).[19]

The twelfth-century *Life of St Elgar* (or *Vita Sancti Elgari*) is the earliest surviving narrative concerning life on Bardsey; it is a simple and beautiful account of the unfolding of a hermit's vocation. It recounts how Elgar was born in Devon and captured by pirates as a child. This is quite plausible; in the second half of the eleventh century, it was normal for Scottish and Welsh kings to capture slaves, who were often deported from Bristol to Ireland. Elgar was sold to an Irish lord, probably in around 1067, and was freed after his master's death, but recaptured by the King of Connaght and made executioner.[20]

The Life describes Elgar's unhappiness in this role:

> Leading such a life, reluctantly and against his will, in grief and sadness and among hostile bands, nevertheless daily awaiting the mercy of God and the release of his body

and soul, he obtained his release and having done penance suitable to his troubled state, leaving the country entirely and mindful of his difficulties, he embarked on a ship and suffered shipwreck.[21]

Early Irish law required a person who had reluctantly committed a crime to be punished; if a man killed another unintentionally, his punishment was commuted to being placed on a boat and set adrift. The author of Elgar's Life appears to refer to this crime, with its punishment.

Elgar was shipwrecked on Bardsey, probably in the early 1090s. Bardsey was an island with which the author of the Life was evidently familiar, for he describes it in some detail:

> [It] is surrounded on all sides by the sea and has a lofty promontory [Mynydd Enlli] on its eastern side, with its western coast level and fertile, with soil irrigated by a sweet fountain, with the maritime part full of dolphins.[22]

Elgar decided to remain on Bardsey with the monks he found there, and the sailors departed. He learnt monastic life by living alongside the monks for seven years:

> Although having been raised untaught and rough, he improved daily in the solitary life. He lived seven years with a community of brethren, sometimes alone, living a holy, glorious, chaste life, with little bread, thin clothing and a worn countenance.[23]

As a result of campaigns by Hugh of Shrewsbury and Hugh of Chester in the early twelfth century, the inhabitants of Gwynedd were evicted and fled, leaving the Llŷn peninsula desolate. Elgar remained on Bardsey, however:

> For a further seven years, while the whole of Gwynedd was desolate, he remained alone in the hermitage, having nothing for his sustenance except what was provided by those creatures succouring him at the will of God.[24]

Elgar's Struggles

The *Life of Elgar* is unique among twelfth-century Lives of the saints in that it focuses not on the miraculous, but on Elgar's actual life. His struggles are described; sometimes he found food, but at other times he went hungry. Once, he found a deer carcass (ch. 8). On another occasion, a huge fish was beached; Elgar tried to kill it but it slipped back into the sea, with Elgar's knife embedded in its side. However, it was beached again on the next tide, complete with Elgar's knife (ch. 7). Sometimes he caught fish that were too unpleasant to eat, but he survived on 'herbs and water and small fish from the sea' (ch. 8).

After seven years, 'master Caradog' came to visit Elgar; the visitor is described as 'learned above all men in the whole of Wales in knowledge of both ancient and new laws' (ch. 4). This might be Caradog of Llancarfan, who compiled much of the *Book of Llandaf*, but it is more likely that Elgar's visitor was Caradog Fynach (d. 1124), a hermit who lived in Glamorgan and Pembrokeshire, whose relics were enshrined at St David's; Gerald of Wales considered him as the most suitable candidate for canonisation among the holy people of Dyfed.[25]

Caradog invited Elgar to leave the island and travel south with him in order to receive 'the solace of food and clothing'. Elgar was uncertain what to do—an easier life was very tempting. He went to his chapel to pray about it, and decided to stay where he was, encouraged by the many holy men who had lived there before him (ch. 9). Elgar dug his own grave, and after his death he was discovered and buried by sailors.

Elgar's Awareness of the Saints

Throughout the Life, Elgar is portrayed as deeply aware of the holy men who preceded him on Bardsey, 'Dubricius [Dyfrig] the Archbishop of western Britain, Daniel, Bishop of the church of Bangor and St Paternus and many others whose bodies are buried in this island' (ch. 5). For seven years, Elgar had lived and prayed with his fellow monks, and he had learnt holiness from them; he still heard their advice ringing in his ears on a daily basis. He was profoundly aware of the communion of saints—he was of the Christian belief that those who have gone before us love and care for us still, now that they are with God.

Elgar took literally the words in the Letter to the Hebrews in the New Testament: 'With so many witnesses in a great cloud on every side of us, we too, then, should throw off everything that hinders us' (Hebrews 12.1). Elgar knew that through his life as a monk on Bardsey he had been brought to live among the saints: 'You have been placed with the spirits of the saints who have been made perfect' (Hebrews 12. 23).

Eastern Orthodox Christians are more conscious of this, perhaps, than those in the West; they believe that when we pray, we stand among the angels and saints. In Orthodox churches, women worship on the left and men on the right, while female saints are painted on the north wall and male saints are depicted on the south wall. In this way, women pray alongside the female saints and men worship beside their male counterparts.

We join in an activity that is more than human. In the twentieth century, Mother Maria, an Orthodox nun, described chanting the psalms in a ramshackle barn at Olney, Bedfordshire, which served as her monastery chapel. It meant:

> …standing happily among the saints and angels, and to sing—in or out of harmony is irrelevant, but to sing and not to fuss about it all being unseen. And *not* to have faith would then mean to stand among them—because one can't escape that—and to sulk.[26]

Monks and nuns are particularly aware, perhaps, of belonging to the communion of saints. Modern Benedictines, who as novices memorise Benedict's Rule, will say 'St Benedict says this or that' and consider themselves to be his disciples, although they are separated from him in time by 1,500 years. If Elgar believed in the communion of saints, his awareness of the presence of Dyfrig, Deiniol, and Padarn—and a host of other monks—would not be extraordinary.

Elgar explained to Caradog that, living alone as he did, it was these 'holy spirits' who gave him comfort. They:

> …constantly, day and night, succoured me as if I were destitute and enfeebled … By these ministrations I know nothing to be wanting in prosperity and joy, and nothing of poverty and penury to be pressing me; always they say to me what is true, always they say to me what is just.[27]

Sometimes they recalled to his mind comforting words from the scriptures:

> They report to me that the present life is like the flower of the field [Matthew 6. 28], the future like an odour of balsam [Song of Songs 4. 14] … so that once the enemy is defeated I should receive the crown and rewards' [James 1. 12; Revelation 2. 10].[28]

Elgar therefore decided to remain on the island.

Chapter 11 of Elgar's Life recounts how, after his death, Bishop Urban of Llandaf authorised the removal from Bardsey of the body of Dyfrig and the teeth of Elgar in 1120, as relics for his cathedral; thus, Llandaf could celebrate its ownership of the 'earliest' Welsh saint, Dyfrig, and its most recent, Elgar the hermit. Elgar's Life was included in the *Book of Llandaf*, alongside a late version of Samson's Life, a Life of Dyfrig, a gospel text, papal bulls, and a collection of charters.

Welsh Hermits

In his *Description of Wales* (1194), Gerald of Wales praises Welsh hermits: 'Nowhere can you see hermits and anchorites more abstinent and more spiritually committed than in Wales'.[29] In Meirionydd, in north Wales, on a list of taxpayers in 1292–3, two women are not only named but their profession is also described. One is a crwth-player (a crwth being a type of harp) and the other, Gwladus, is termed *religiosa*; she is likely to have been a solitary, since there was no community of nuns in Meirionydd.[30]

While there were a number of books—particularly the *Institutes* and *Conferences* of John Cassian—that taught monks and nuns how to live together in monasteries, there were no equivalent texts for hermits. Elgar trained for his solitary vocation by spending seven years living in or on the edge of a community. During the next sixty or so years, a guidebook for hermits was written, probably in the Welsh Borders. It is concerned with both the inner life of solitaries and the many practical details of their external life, and is named *Guide for Anchoresses*.

Guide for Anchoresses

The *Ancren Wisse*, or *Guide for Anchoresses*, was perhaps written in the 1220s in the Welsh Marches, in a West Midlands dialect, with a large element of Old Norse and a sprinkling of

Welsh. The manuscript may have been written at Wigmore Abbey, a few miles south-west of Ludlow, in northern Herefordshire; this was a daughter house of the Augustinian abbey of St Victor in Paris. The book consists of a long and elaborate outline of the daily life of an anchoress, with observances for her to follow and advice for holy living.[31]

Ancren Wisse appears to have been written by the spiritual guide or guides of a group of anchoresses, and is both affectionate and urgent in tone. It is one of six elegant books, compact enough to be easily held in the hand, written neatly and clearly on good parchment. All appear to have been written between 1200 and 1230; the works borrow from and refer to each other.[32] The quality of their English prose was unequalled for over a century, at a time when most literary texts were written in Latin or in Anglo-Norman French.[33]

The three nuns and their servants seem to have been generously supported by their patron, although this was not a common situation. In one version of *Ancren Wisse*, the author comments:

> I know no other anchoress who can get all she needs with greater ease or with greater honour than you three have, our Lord be thanked. For you do not think at all about food or clothing, either for you or for your maidens [i.e. servants]. Each of you has everything you need from a single friend [i.e. patron]; nor need your maidens look further for bread or food than at his hall. God knows it, many others know little of this ease but are very often tormented by deprivation, humiliation and difficulty.[34]

The three women were evidently high-born sisters from the same family, who became anchoresses at a young age; since women married young, if they chose celibacy then this choice had to be made in their early teens.

Ancren Wisse became very popular; copies were made in various parts of England until the end of the fifteenth century. Seventeen manuscripts survive in French, Latin, and English. The work draws on many sources—Augustine, Jerome, Cassian, Gregory, Anselm and Bernard.[35] Its focus on the teachings of Cassian and the Desert Mothers and Fathers connects the nuns for whom *Ancren Wisse* was written with the vowed men and women of early medieval times.

Desert Spirituality

In his introduction to *Ancren Wisse*, the author enumerates some of the Desert Mothers and Fathers whom the three anchoresses could take as models for holiness:

> Paul the first anchorite, Anthony and Arsenius … Also St Sarah and St Syncletica and many other such men and women with their rough sleeping-mats and their harsh hair shirts.[36]

While the gospels provided a rule of life for early monks and nuns, the Desert Mothers and Fathers formed a vital link with the gospels, and many of the 'Sayings of the Desert Fathers' echo the words of Jesus.

In Part 3 of *Ancren Wisse*, the author comments on Christ's admonition, 'If anyone hits you on the right cheek, offer him the other as well' (Mt. 5. 38). He gives an example of such an attitude from *The Lives of the Desert Fathers*:

> Think how the holy man in 'The Lives of the Fathers' kissed and blessed the hand of the other one who had harmed him, and said most earnestly, while kissing it eagerly, 'Blessed be this hand for ever, for it has [brought] me the joys of heaven'.[37]

Every experience, good or bad, can be put to good use. The author of *Ancren Wisse* quotes a saying of another Desert Father, Abba Moses, to emphasise this:

> As the holy abbot Moses said, all the woe and all the hardship we suffer in the flesh, and all the good that we ever do, all such things are nothing except as [it were] tools with which to cultivate the heart.[38]

This saying of Abba Moses is told by John Cassian in his *Conferences*. Many monasteries would have a copy of this work, with its observations on how to live a holy life. Cassian went to Egypt in around 385 and spent fifteen years learning from the Desert Mothers and Fathers. After a further twenty years of reflection on his experience, he wrote his *Conferences* to explain the aims and methods of monastic life.

Virtues and Vices

Like other medieval guides to holy living, the *Ancren Wisse* analyses behaviour according to the categories developed by the Desert Fathers and organised by Cassian, based upon the 'seven deadly sins' and their remedies. The author of *Ancren Wisse* adds a new layer of homely imagery to this traditional teaching, however. With a touch of humour, he recommends a thorough approach to confessing sins. His three friends should be like a widow turning out her house; she makes a huge pile of the dirt, and gets rid of it. Then she gathers up the remaining dirt and gets rid of that. Finally, she sweeps the dust away:

> When the poor widow wants to clean her house, she first of all gathers all the dust in a heap, and then sweeps it out. Then she comes back and heaps what has been left together again, and sweeps it out after. After that, if it is very dusty, she sprinkles water on the fine dust and sweeps it out after all the rest. In the same way, one who confesses must push out the small sins after the great ones.[39]

This imagery is based on the gospel parable of the widow who loses a precious coin and then lights a lamp, sweeps the house, and searches her home until she finds the coin, after which she celebrates with her friends (Luke 15. 8–10). Much of what the nuns are to 'sweep out' is simple and ordinary:

…too much or too little food or drink, grumbling, a grim face, sitting too long at the parlour window [to gossip], hours [liturgical prayers] poorly said or without attention of the heart or at the wrong time … scornful laughter, or letting things grow mouldy, rusty or rotten; leaving clothes unmended, wet with rain, or unwashed.

But there should be no punishment:

The priest need not for any fault, unless it be very great, impose any other penance upon you than the life which you lead according to this rule.[40]

There is also a new pragmatism—not every priest is wise enough to give advice. One should seek out a prudent man, carefully chosen:

Confession of secret sin must always be prudent, and made to a wise man, and not to young priests—I mean young of wit—nor to a stupid old one.[41]

Enclosure

A new element in vowed life was the enclosure of solitaries within their anchorhold. The author encourages the three women to think of this as a temporary situation, like Jesus confined within Mary's womb, or buried in the tomb before his resurrection:

The womb was a narrow dwelling, where our Lord was a recluse…. If you then suffer bitterness in a narrow place, you are his fellows, recluse as he was in Mary's womb. Are you imprisoned within four wide walls? So was he in a narrow cradle, nailed on the cross, enclosed tight in a stone tomb. Mary's womb and this tomb were his anchorhouses.[42]

To compensate for their confinement, they are promised great freedom in heaven:

All who are in heaven shall be as swift as man's thought now is, and as the sunbeam that darts from east to west, and as the eye opens and shuts…. [You] shall play in heaven in such wide confines—as it is said that in heaven is large pasture—that the body shall be wherever the spirit wills, in an instant. Now this is the one special gift which I say that anchoresses shall have more than others.

Radical Commitment

Jesus demanded radical commitment from his disciples. When a young man asked to follow him, but wanted to first say goodbye to his family, Jesus retorted: 'Leave the dead to bury their dead' (Matthew 8. 22). In his *Conferences*, Cassian quotes one of the Desert Fathers who used similar language. The author of *Ancren Wisse* repeats what Cassian wrote:

There was once a religious man, and his natural brother came to him for help, and he referred him on to his third brother, who was dead and buried. The brother answered wonderingly. 'No!' he said, 'Is he not dead?' 'And so am I,' said the holy man: 'Dead to the world'. The author comments: Family feeling is not proper for an anchoress.[43]

This teaching sounds radical, but it formed the essence of discipleship as early monks and nuns saw it. Many of them felt called to leave their country 'for the love of God', to leave their tribal home as a pilgrim for Christ. The three women hermits for whom *Ancren Wisse* was written were unlikely to travel, but in their hearts they were free from worldly ties. At least, this is what they desired, and this is what they would try to share with others who came to them for support and encouragement on their own journey through life.

A Paradox

Single vowed life is a paradox that celibate monks and nuns have always tried to explore. Is giving up everything really worth it? Is it worth seeking a God who so often hides his face? It is not easy to sustain a relationship with an elusive God. The author of *Ancren Wisse* knows that his three women friends will sometimes lose heart. He uses homely language to encourage them; they are children of God, our mother, who plays a game of hide-and-seek with us:

Our Lord, when he allows us to be tempted, is playing with us like a mother with her young darling; she runs away from him and hides herself, and lets him sit alone and look eagerly about, crying 'Mother! Mother!' and crying for a while, and then with open arms she jumps out laughing, and hugs and kisses him, and wipes his eyes.... At the same moment our Lord loves us none the less, for he does it out of his great love.[44]

The author also offers a great deal of practical advice. A common means of preventing or curing disease at this time was bloodletting, the withdrawal of small quantities of blood; this was thought to balance the four humours of Ancient Greek medicine, which corresponded to four temperaments—sanguine, choleric, melancholic, and phlegmatic. If an anchoress was bled, then she should relax afterwards:

When you are finished letting blood, you must do nothing that is difficult for three days, but talk to your maidens and amuse yourselves together with virtuous stories. You may do so whenever you feel heavy or are sad or sick.[45]

Ancren Wisse is a lengthy work that must have taken a long time to compile. Its author ends by saying that a pilgrimage to Rome would have been easier than the effort and labour of writing it:

Read from this book in your leisure time every day, much or little. I hope that it will be very profitable to you, if you read it often, through God's grace—or else I have badly wasted my long hours. God knows, I would rather set out for Rome than start it over again! [46]

There is a new tone to this writing; it is rooted in traditional monastic values, but expressed in a modern language which values normality, playfulness, and human feelings. The work has an almost contemporary ring—its style is more everyday and less supernatural. The search for sainthood is placed in a new context; there is a humanism here that heralds the dawn of a new era.

Endnotes

Part I: Saints of South Wales

Chapter One

1. *Gildas: The Ruin of Britain and Other Works*, transl. M. Winterbottom (Chichester: Phillimore, 1978), 'The Ruin of Britain', ch. 10.
2. W. H. Davies, 'The Church in Wales', in M. W. Barley and R. P. Hanson, eds., *Christianity in Britain, 300-700, Papers presented to the Conference on Christianity in Roman and Sub-Roman Britain, held at the University of Nottingham, 17-20 April 1967* (Leicester: Leicester University Press, 1967), p. 140.
3. M. Costen, *The Origins of Somerset* (Manchester: Manchester University Press, 1992) p. 74.
4. *Gildas: The Ruin of Britain*, 11.
5. *The Life of Martin of Tours* by Sulpicius Severus, ch. 10, in J. P. Migne, *Patrologia Latina*, vol. 20, (Paris, 1844-64), columns 159-222.
6. N. Russell, *The Lives of the Desert Fathers*, Prologue, 10 (London: Mowbray, 1981), p. 50.
7. N. Russell, *The Lives of the Desert Fathers*, pp. 13, 18, 53.
8. Sulpicius Severus, *The Life of Martin of Tours*, ch. 10.
9. 2 Kgs. 2. 1–18; Jn. 1. 35-9.
10. *Carmina XVI* in W. B. Anderson, *Sidonius: Poems and Letters,* Bks. I-II, (Cambridge, Massachusetts: Harvard University Press, 1963), p. 250, modernised by the author.
11. *Tescua quidam putant esse tuguria, quidam loca praerupta et aspera*, Etym. XX, in *The Etymologies of Isidore of Seville*, transl. S. A. Barney, W. J. Lewis, J. A. Beach, O. Berghof (Cambridge: Cambridge University Press, 2006).
12. *The Life of Saint David* by Rhygyfarch, ed. and transl. R. Sharpe and J. R. Davies, chs. 41, 43, in *St David of Wales: Cult, Church and Nation*, Studies in Celtic History, vol. 24, ed. J. Wyn Evans and J. M. Wooding (Woodbridge: The Boydell Press, 2007). Modomnóc also had a cult in Wexford. His principal church was at Tipperaghney in Kilkenny, in the territory of the Osraige. See Sharpe and Davies p. 137, n. 80.
13. E. Herbert McAvoy, 'Anchorites and medieval Wales', in *Anchoritic Traditions of Medieval Europe*, ed. E. Herbert McAvoy (Woodbridge: The Boydell Press, 2010), p. 209.

14. The excavations were carried out by the University of Wales, Trinity and St David, with the Dyfed Archaeological Trust. See P. Wilkinson, 'Dig reveals medieval Welsh convent', *Church Times*, 18. 7. 2014.

15. A hexagonal honeycomb was also easy to depict on mosaics. For a study of Judaeo-Christian symbolism, see I. Mancini, *Archaeological Discoveries Relative to the Judaeo-Christians*, Studium Biblicum Franciscanum Collectio Minor no. 10 (Jerusalem: Franciscan Printing Press, 1984).

16. Scriptural quotations are from *The Jerusalem Bible*, ed. A. Jones (London: Darton, Longman and Todd, 1968), except for the psalms, which are taken from *The Psalms: a new translation* (London: Collins Fontana, 1967).

17. Rufinus, *Historium Monachorum in Aegypto*, in J. P. Migne (ed.), *Patrologia Latina* (Paris, 1844-64), vol. 21, columns 387-462.

18. '*Félire Óengusso Céli Dé*: the Martyrology of Oengus the Culdee', ed. and transl. W. Stokes (London: Henry Bradshaw Society, 1905; reprint, 1984), p. 60.

19. I am grateful to Professor Thomas O'Loughlin, at Nottingham University, for this observation.

20. *The Life of Saint David* by Rhygyfarch, ch. 43, ed. and transl. R. Sharpe and J. R. Davies in *St David of Wales: Cult, Church and Nation*, pp. 138-9.

21. H. Sykes, *Celtic Britain* (London: Phoenix, 1998), p. 133.

22. O. Davies, *Celtic Christianity in Early Medieval Wales* (Cardiff: University of Wales Press, 1996), pp. 29-30.

23. O. Davies, *Celtic Christianity in Early Medieval Wales*, pp. 45-6.

24. At Roscrea in Ireland, *Céli Dé* formed a separate community adjoining an unreformed one, while at Armagh they formed a group within the monastic enclosure.

25. O. Davies, *Celtic Christianity in Early Medieval Wales*, pp. 47-8, 64.

26. O. Davies, *Celtic Christianity in Early Medieval Wales*, pp. 49-50.

27. A. O. H. Jarman, *Llyfr Du Caerfyrddin* (Cardiff: University of Wales Press, 1982), p. 9.

28. O. Davies, *Celtic Christianity in Early Medieval Wales*, p. 66.

Chapter Two

1. H. James, 'The geography of the cult of St David: a study of dedication patterns in the medieval diocese', in *St David of Wales: Cult, Church and Nation*, Studies in Celtic History 24, ed. J. Wyn Evans and J. M. Wooding (Woodbridge: The Boydell Press, 2007) p. 47.

2. J. M. Wooding, 'The Figure of David', in *St David of Wales: Cult, Church and Nation*, p. 11.

3. J. R. Davies, 'Some observations on the 'Nero', 'Digby', and 'Vespasian' recensions of *Vita S. David*', in *St David of Wales: Cult, Church and Nation*, pp. 159-60.

4. J. R. Davies, 'Some observations', p. 159.

5. J. Cartwright, 'The Cult of St Non: rape, sanctity and motherhood in Welsh and Breton hagiography', in *St David of Wales: Cult, Church and Nation*, p. 185.

6. J. R. Davies, 'Some observations', p. 160.

7. E. G. Bowen, *The St David of History. Dewi Sant: Our Founder Saint* (Aberystwyth: Friends of St David's Cathedral, 1982), pp. 9-10.

8. H. James, 'The geography of the cult of St David', p. 76.

9. O. Davies, *Celtic Christianity in Early Medieval Wales* (Cardiff: University of Wales Press, 1996), p. 23.

10. 'The Life of Saint David by Rhygyfarch', chs. 49, 52, ed. and transl. R. Sharpe and J. R. Davies in *St David of Wales: Cult, Church and Nation*, pp. 143-7.

11. H. James, 'The geography of the cult of St David', pp. 77-8.

12. H. James, 'The geography of the cult of St David', p. 77.

13. D. Dumville, 'Saint David of Wales', Kathleen Hughes Memorial Lecture on Medieval Welsh History, 2002, reprinted in D. Dumville, *Celtic Essays, 2001-2007* (Aberdeen: Centre for Celtic Studies, University of Aberdeen, 2007).

14. J. M. Wooding, 'The Figure of David', in *St David of Wales: Cult, Church and Nation*, p. 16.

15. J. M. Wooding, 'The Figure of David', p. 14.

16. Asser, *Vita Aelfredi Regis* 79, transl. in *Alfred the Great. Asser's Life of King Alfred and other contemporary sources*, S. D. Keynes and M. Lapidge (Harmondsworth: Penguin, 1983), pp. 94-6.

17. H. James, 'The geography of the cult of St David', p. 47.

18. J. Wyn Evans, 'Transition and survival: St David and St Davids Cathedral', in *St David of Wales: Cult, Church and Nation*, pp. 32-3.

19. J. Wyn Evans, 'Transition and survival', p. 33.

20. H. James, 'The cult of St David in the Middle Ages', in *In Search of a Cult: Essays in Honour of Philip Rahtz*, ed. M. Carver (Woodbridge: Boydell & Brewer, 1992), pp. 105-6.

21. E. R. Henken, 'Welsh hagiography and the nationalist impulse' in *Celtic Hagiography and saints' cults*, ed. J. Cartwright (Cardiff: University of Wales Press, 2003), p. 43, n. 50.

22. *The* Brut y Twysogyon, *or, The Chronicle of the Princes, Red Book of Hergest Version*, ed. and transl. T. Jones (Cardiff: University of Wales Press, 2nd ed., 1973), ch. 33.

23. Ch. 155, quoted in H. James, 'The cult of St David in the Middle Ages', p. 110.

24. *Vita Griffini Filii Conani: The Medieval Latin Life of Gruffudd Ap Cynan*, ed. and transl. P. Russell (Cardiff: University of Wales Press, 2006).

25. J. Sampson, 'The History of the Shrine', in *A Shrine Restored*, ed. H. Williams (St Davids: Red Dot Design Publications, 2012), pp. 4-5.

26. H. James, 'The cult of St David in the Middle Ages', pp. 110-11.

27. T. Wright, ed., 'Letters Relating to the Suppression of the Monasteries', Camden Society, vol. 26, 1843, p.184, quoted in 'The History of the Shrine' by J. Sampson, pp. 8-9.

28. F. Jones, *The Holy Wells of Wales* (Cardiff: University of Wales Press, 1992), p. 27.

29. E. G. Bowen, *The St David of History*, pp. 15-16.

30. Browne Willis, *A Survey of the Cathedral Church of St David's* (London, 1717), pp. 52-3.

31. R. Fenton, *Historical Tour through Pembrokeshire* (Brecknock: Fenton, 1903), pp. 63-4.

32. J. Cartwright, 'The Cult of St Non', pp. 204-5.

33. P. Ó Riain, 'The Saints of Cardiganshire', in *From Earliest Times to the Coming of the Normans: Cardiganshire County History*, vol. 1, ed. J. L. Davies and D. P. Kirby (Cardiff: University of Wales Press, 1994), p. 394.

34. J. Cartwright, 'The Cult of St Non', pp. 182-3, 203.

35. J. Cartwright, 'The Cult of St Non', p. 205.

36. Paris, Bibliothèque Nationale de France, fonds celtique 5.

37. 'Buez Santez Nonn hac ez map Deuy', ed. and transl. Y. Le Berre, in *Buez santez Nonn. Vie de sainte Nonne. Mystère breton*, ed. Y. Le Berre, B. Tanguy and Y.-P. Castel (Brest: CRBC, Minihi-Levenez, 1999), pp. 113-94.

38. B. Tanguy, 'The cults of Ss. Nonne and Divi in Brittany', in *St David of Wales: Cult, Church and Nation*, pp. 196-7.

39. P. Ó Riain, 'The Saints of Cardiganshire', p. 390.

40. H. James, 'The geography of the cult of St David', p. 76.

41. N. Ludlow, 'CADW: Welsh Monuments. Early Medieval Ecclesiastical Sites Project: Ceredigion', Cambria Archaeology, Appendix 2, 2002.

42. J. Meyrick, *A Pilgrim's Guide to the Holy Wells of Cornwall* (Falmouth: Meyrick, 1982), p. 15.

43. N. Orme, *The Saints of Cornwall* (Oxford: Oxford University Press, 2000), pp. 207-8.

44. J. Meyrick, *A Pilgrim's Guide*, pp. 119-20.

45. H. James, 'The geography of the cult of St David', p. 49.

46. H. James, 'The cult of St David in the Middle Ages', p. 107

47. E. J. Boake, 'Report on the excavation of the Chapel of St Justinian, St Davids', *Archaeologia Cambrensis*, vol. 81, 1926.

48. D. Petts, *The Early Medieval Church in Wales* (Stroud: The History Press, 2009), pp. 62-3.

49. H. James, 'The geography of the cult of St David', p. 50.

50. H. James, 'The geography of the cult of St David', p. 50.

Chapter Three

1. T. Roberts, 'English Ecclesiastical Place-Names and Archaeology', in *The Early Church in Wales and the West*, ed. N. Edwards and A. Lane, Oxbow Monograph 16 (Oxford: Oxbow Books, 1992), pp. 43-4.

2. D. Petts, *The Early Medieval Church in Wales* (Stroud: The History Press, 2009), pp. 124-5, 191.

3. D. Petts, *The Early Medieval Church in Wales*, pp. 90, 188.

4. J. Wyn Evans, 'The Survival of the *Clas* as an Institution in Medieval Wales: Some Observations on Llanbadarn Fawr', in *The Early Church in Wales and the West*, p. 33.

5. Gerald of Wales, *Itinerarium Cambriae* (*Journey Through Wales*) (1191), bk. 2. ch. 5, transl. L. Thorpe (Harmondsworth: Penguin, 1978).

6. D. Petts, *The Early Medieval Church in Wales*, p. 172.

7. D. Howlett, 'A triad of texts about St David', in *St David of Wales: Cult, Church and Nation*, Studies in Celtic History vol. 24, ed. J. Wyn Evans and J. M. Wooding (Woodbridge: The Boydell Press, 2007), p. 253.

8. J. R. Davies, 'Some observations on the 'Nero', 'Digby', and 'Vespasian' recensions of *Vita S. David*', in *St David of Wales: Cult, Church and Nation*, p. 159.

9. Rhygyfarch's *Life of David*, ch. 64, transl. R. Sharpe in 'Rhygyfarch's "Life" of David' by R. Sharpe and J. R. Davies, in *St David of Wales: Cult, Church and Nation*, p. 151.

10. D. Petts, *The Early Medieval Church in Wales*, p. 96.

11. D. Petts, *The Early Medieval Church in Wales*, p. 96.

12. D. Howlett, 'A triad of texts about St David', p. 253.

13. D. Howlett, 'A triad of texts about St David', pp. 253-4.

14. D. Howlett, 'A triad of texts about St David', pp. 255-8.

15. Rhygyfarch's Life of David, ch. 11, transl. R. Sharpe, p. 119.

16. D. Petts, *The Early Medieval Church in Wales*, pp. 141, 143.

17. D. Petts, *The Early Medieval Church in Wales*, p. 141.

18. Life of Brynach, ch. 7, BM Cotton MS Vespasian A xiv, in *Vitae Sanctorum Britanniae et Genealogiae*, ed. A. W. Wade-Evans, (Cardiff: University of Wales Press Board, 1944).

19. K. Jankulak, 'Alba Longa in the Celtic regions? Swine, saints and Celtic hagiography' in *Celtic Hagiography and Saints' Cults*, ed. J. Cartwright (Cardiff: University of Wales Press, 2003), pp. 272-81.

20. K. Jankulak, 'Alba Longa in the Celtic regions?', pp. 277-8.

21. C. Guest, transl., *The Mabinogion* (Mineola, New York: Dover Publications, 1997), pp. 38-9.

22. H. James, 'The geography of the cult of St David: a study of dedication patterns in the medieval diocese', in *St David of Wales: Cult, Church and Nation'*, p. 51.

23. F. Jones, *The Holy Wells of Wales* (Cardiff: Cardiff University Press, 1992), p. 43.

24. J. Wyn Evans, 'Transition and survival: St David and St Davids Cathedral', in *St David of Wales: Cult, Church and Nation*, pp. 27-8.

25. D. Petts, *The Early Medieval Church in Wales*, p. 163.

26. J. Sharkey, *Celtic High Crosses of Wales* (Llanrwst: Gwasg Carreg Gwalch, 1998), pp. 116-7.

27. Folio 141, quoted in W. M. Lindsay, *Early Welsh Script*, (Oxford: Oxford University Press, 1912).

28. D. Brown, *The Lichfield Gospels* (London: Pitkin, 1982), p. 6.

29. D. Petts, *The Early Medieval Church in Wales*, p. 93.

30. R. Gameson, 'The insular gospel book at Hereford Cathedral', *Scriptorium* no. 56, 2002.

31. D. Petts, *The Early Medieval Church in Wales*, pp. 95-6.

32. D. Petts, *The Early Medieval Church in Wales*, pp. 107-8.

33. R. Gameson, 'The insular gospel book at Hereford Cathedral'.

Chapter Four

1. Prologue to the Life of Samson, from T. Taylor, *The Life of St Samson of Dol* (London, SPCK, 1925), emended by K. Jankulak from the Latin text of P. Flobert, *La vie ancienne de saint Samson de Dol* (Paris: CNRS Éditions, 1997).

2. O. Davies, *Celtic Christianity in Early Medieval Wales* (Cardiff: University of Wales Press, 1996), p. 13.

3. O. Davies, *Celtic Christianity in Early Medieval Wales*, p. 14.

4. *The Life of Samson*, ch. 7, T. Taylor, *The Life of St Samson of Dol*.

5. *The Life of Samson*, ch. 10, T. Taylor, *The Life of St Samson of Dol*.

6. *The Life of Samson*, ch. 21, T. Taylor, *The Life of St Samson of Dol*.

7. *The Life of Samson*, ch. 34, T. Taylor, *The Life of St Samson of Dol*.

8. *The Life of Samson*, ch. 36, T. Taylor, *The Life of St Samson of Dol*.

9. *The Life of Samson*, chs. 40-41, T. Taylor, *The Life of St Samson of Dol*.

10. *Vita Antoniae*, ch. 14, in J. P. Migne, *Patrologia Graeca* (Paris, 1857-66), vol. 26, cols. 839-975, transl. M. Groves and R. Walls, in *Life of Saint Antony* (Vauve: Aide Inter-Monastères, 1994), p. 32.

11. *The Life of Samson*, ch. 42, T. Taylor, *The Life of St Samson of Dol*.

12. D. Petts, *The Early Medieval Church in Wales* (Stroud: The History Press, 2009), p. 76.

13. D. Petts, *The Early Medieval Church in Wales*, pp. 96, 127.

14. D. Petts, *The Early Medieval Church in Wales*, p. 38.

15. M. Redknap, *The Christian Celts: Treasures of Late Celtic Wales* (Cardiff: National Museum of Wales, 1991), p. 44.

16. D. Petts, *The Early Medieval Church in Wales*, pp. 31-2, 127, 182.

17. *The Life of Samson*, ch. 45, T. Taylor, *The Life of St Samson of Dol*.

18. B. Merdrignac, 'The process and significance of rewriting in Breton hagiography', in *Celtic Hagiography and saints' cults*, ed. J. Cartwright (Cardiff: University of Wales Press, 2003), p. 194.

19. J. R. Davies, *The Book of Llandaf and the Norman Church in Wales* (Woodbridge: The Boydell Press, 2003), p. 10.

20. D. Petts, *The Early Medieval Church in Wales*, pp. 49, 163, 167.

21. E. G. Bowen, *The Settlements of the Celtic Saints in Wales* (Cardiff: University of Wales Press, 1954), p. 36.

22. T. Roberts, 'Welsh Ecclesiastical Place-names and Archaeology' in N. Edwards and A. Lane (eds), *The Early Church in Wales and the West* (Oxford: Oxbow Books, 1992), Oxbow Monographs no. 16, p. 43.

23. Life of Dyfrig, ch. 5, J. G. Evans and J. Rhys, eds., *The text of the Book of Llan Dâv reproduced from the Gwysaney Manuscript* (1893), facs. ed. Aberystwyth: University of Wales Press, 1979.

24. K. Jankulak, 'Alba Longa in the Celtic regions? Swine, saints and Celtic hagiography' in *Celtic Hagiography and Saints' Cults*, ed. J. Cartwright (Cardiff: University of Wales Press, 2003), p. 274.

25. D. Petts, *The Early Medieval Church in Wales*, pp. 171, 177.

26. D. Brook, 'The Early Christian Church East and West of Offa's Dyke', in *The Early Church in Wales and the West*, p. 79.

27. Harl. MS 6726, quoted in D. Petts, *The Early Medieval Church in Wales*, p. 73.

28. 'The Life of St Elgar of Ynys Enlli', transl. and ed. K. Jankulak and J. M. Wooding, in *Solitaries, Pastors and 20,000 Saints—Studies in the Religious History of Ynys Enlli (Bardsey Island)*, ed. J. M. Wooding (Lampeter: Trivium Publications, 2010).

39. O. Davies, *Celtic Christianity in Early Medieval Wales*, p. 12.

Chapter Five

1. H. James, 'Early Medieval Cemeteries in Wales', in *The Early Church in Wales and the West*, ed. N. Edwards and A. Lane (Oxford: Oxbow Books, 1992), Oxbow Monograph 16, p. 96.

2. D. Petts, *The Early Medieval Church in Wales* (Stroud: The History Press, 2009), pp. 159, 161.

3. C. F. Mawer, *Evidence for Christianity in Roman Britain: The Small Finds* (Oxford: Tempus Reparatum, British Archaeological Reports, 1995), British Series no. 243.

4. N. Edwards and A. Lane, 'The Archaeology of the Early Church in Wales: an Introduction', in *The Early Church in Wales and the West*, p. 8.

5. N. Edwards and A. Lane, 'The Archaeology of the Early Church in Wales', p. 8.

6. A. Seaman, *Trial Excavation at Mount St Albans, near Caerleon, May 2008* (MA diss., Cardiff University, 2010), pp. 1-2.

7. *De Situ Brecheniauc* and *Cognacio Brychan*, in P. C. Bartrum, *The Early Welsh Genealogical Tracts*, MFU 4567 (Cardiff: University of Wales Press, 1966), and Jesus College MS 20.

8. Clwyd-Powys Archaeological Trust (CPAT), *Historic Landscape Characterisation. The Making of the Middle Usk Valley Landscape*, 2013.

9. Published respectively in *Revue Celtique* (1870-1934), vol. 5, pp. 413-60, and in *Analecta Bollandiana*, vol. 1, (Brussels: Societé des Bollandistes, 1882-1961) pp. 208-58.

10. G. H. Doble, 'Saint Paulinus of Wales', in *Lives of the Welsh Saints*, ed. D. S. Evans (Cardiff: University of Wales Press, 1971).

11. G. H. Doble, 'Saint Paulinus of Wales'.

12. V. Nash-Williams, *The Early Christian Monuments of Wales* (Cardiff: University of Wales Press, 1950), no. 139, pp. 107-9, plate X, fig. 109; see also N. Edwards, *A Corpus of Early Medieval Inscribed Stones and Stone Sculpture in Wales*, vol. 2 (Cardiff: University of Wales Press, 2007), p. 22. Site: CNWYL/1-UCL.

13. V. Nash-Williams, *The Early Christian Monuments of Wales*, no. 63, Plates Ii, VI, fig. 36. Site: CBRNW/1/1.

14. D. Petts, *The Early Medieval Church in Wales*, p. 106.

15. P. Lord, *The Visual Culture of Wales: Medieval Vision* (Cardiff: University of Wales Press, 2003), p. 24.

16. 'The Life of Saint David by Rhygyfarch', chs. 10, 11, ed. and transl. R. Sharpe and J. R. Davies, in *St David of Wales: Cult, Church and Nation*, Studies in Celtic History 24, ed. J. Wyn Evans and J. M. Wooding (Woodbridge: The Boydell Press, 2007), p. 119.

17. 'The Life of Saint David by Rhygyfarch', ch. 49, p. 143.

18. D. Petts, *The Early Medieval Church in Wales*, pp. 29, 196.

19. Clwyd-Powys Archaeological Trust (CPAT), *Historic Landscape Characterisation*, HCA 1174, 2013.

20. S. Taylor, *The Anglo-Saxon Chronicle: A Collaborative Edition, 4, MS B* (Cambridge: Cambridge University Press, 1983). MS B, the Abingdon Chronicle I, is found in BL Cotton Tiberius A.vi, and dates from the second half of the tenth century.

21. M. Redknap, *The Christian Celts: Treasures of Late Celtic Wales* (Cardiff: National Museum of Wales, 1991), pp. 16, 24.

22. M. Redknap, *The Christian Celts*, p. 16.

23. D. Petts, *The Early Medieval Church in Wales*, pp. 105, 107.

24. M. Redknap, *The Christian Celts*, p. 24.

25. *Vita Cadoci*, ed. and transl. A. W. Wade-Evans, in *Vitae Sanctorum Britanniae et Genealogiae* (Cardiff: University of Wales Press Board, 1944), pp. 24-141.

26. K. Jankulak, 'Alba Longa in the Celtic regions? Swine, saints and Celtic hagiography', in *Celtic Hagiography and Saints' Cults*, ed. J. Cartwright (Cardiff: University of Wales Press, 2003), pp. 273-4.

27. I am grateful to J. Wyn Evans, Bishop of St David's Cathedral, for this observation.

28. D. Petts, *The Early Medieval Church in Wales*, pp. 175, 186.

29. M. Priziac, *Bretagne des Saintes et des Croyances* (Grâces-Guingamp: Ki-Dour Éditions, 2002), pp. 97-101.

30. D. Petts, *The Early Medieval Church in Wales*, pp. 45, 108, 184.

31. Quoted in D. Petts, *The Early Medieval Church in Wales*, p. 150.

32. V. Nash-Williams, *The Early Christian Monuments of Wales*, nos. 207, 208.

33. F. Jones, *The Holy Wells of Wales* (Cardiff: University of Wales Press, 1992), p. 204.

34. E. Evans, *CADW: Early medieval ecclesiastical sites in southeast Wales* (The Glamorgan-Gwent Archaeological Trust, 2003), p. 13.

35. T. Roberts, 'Welsh Ecclesiastical Place-Names and Archaeology', in *The Early Church in Wales and the West*, p. 42.

Part II: Saints of North Wales

Chapter Six

1. C. McKenna, ed., 'Canu Cadfan', ll. 50-51, in K. A. Bramley et al (eds), *Gwaith Llewelyn Fardd I*, pp. 9-32 (Cardiff: University of Wales Press, 1994).

2. F. Jones, *The Holy Wells of Wales* (Cardiff: University of Wales Press, 1992), p. 191.

3. *Canu Cadfan*, transl. C. McKenna, in 'The Hagiographic poetics of *Canu Cadfan*' in K. Klar et al (ed), *A Celtic Florilegium* (Oxford: Oxbow Books, 1997), ll. 25-8.

4. N. A. Jones and M. E. Owen, 'Twelfth-century Welsh hagiography: the *Gogynfeirdd* poems to saints', in *Celtic Hagiography and saints' cults*, ed. J. Cartwright (Cardiff: University of Wales Press, 2003), pp. 45-6.

5. C. McKenna, ed., 'Canu Cadfan', p. 17, ll. 18-22.

6. N. A. Jones and M. E. Owen, 'Twelfth-century Welsh hagiography', p. 57.

7. N. A. Jones and M. E. Owen, 'Twelfth-century Welsh hagiography', pp. 57-8; note 110.

8. C. McKenna, ed., 'Canu Cadfan', p. 19, ll. 115-22.

9. O. Davies, *Celtic Christianity in Early Medieval Wales* (Cardiff: University of Wales Press, 1996), pp. 144, 93.

10. C. McKenna, ed. and transl., *The Medieval Welsh Religious Lyric—Poems Of The Gogynfeirdd, 1137-1282* (Belmont, Massachusetts: Ford & Bailie, 1991), p. 16.

11. Information at St Trillo's chapel, Llandrillo-yn-Rhos, 2014.

12. F. Jones, *The Holy Wells of Wales*, pp. 116, 190.

13. D. Petts, *The Early Medieval Church in Wales* (Stroud: The History Press, 2009), pp. 179, 191.

14. C. Knightly, *Mwynhewch Sir Ddinbych Ganoloesol* (Denbigh: Cyngor Sir Ddinbych, 1998), p. 18.

15. C. Fisher, 'The Welsh Celtic Bells', in *Archaeologia Cambrensis*, vol. 81, no. 2, 1926.

16. F. Jones, *The Holy Wells of Wales*, p. 178.

17. D. Petts, *The Early Medieval Church in Wales*, p. 73.

18. P. Owen, ed., transl., 'Canu Tysilio Sant', in N. A. Jones and P. Owen, eds, *Gwaith Cynddelw Brydydd Mawr*, vol. 1 (Cardiff: University of Wales Press, 1991), pp. 15-50.

19. D. Petts, *The Early Medieval Church in Wales*, pp. 155, 141.

20. N. A. Jones and M. E. Owen, 'Twelfth-century Welsh hagiography', p. 49.

21. P. Owen ed., transl., 'Canu Tysilio Sant', p. 32, ll. 148-54.

22. N. A. Jones and M. E. Owen, 'Twelfth-century Welsh hagiography', pp. 60, 66.

23. Thomas Pennard, *A Journal of a tour through north Wales in the year 1792* (pub. Thomas Jenner, n.d.).

24. 'The Life of St Melangell' ed. O. Davies, in *Celtic Spirituality*, The Classics of Western Spirituality Series (New Jersey: Paulist Press, 1999), p. 221.

25. 'The Life of St Melangell', p. 222.

26. CPAT (Clwyd-Powys Archaeological Trust), *Historic Landscape Characterisation. The Tanat Valley: Cwm Pennant, Llangynog, Powys*, HLCA 1011, 2014.

27. W. Britnell and N. Jones, 'Pennant Melangell, Llangynog', *Archaeology in Wales*, 1989, vol. 29, pp. 63-4.

28. N. Edwards and A. Lane, 'The Archaeology of the Early Church in Wales: an Introduction', in *The Early Church in Wales and the West*, ed. N. Edwards and A. Lane (Oxford: Oxbow Books, 1992), Oxbow Monograph 16, p. 10.

29. CPAT, *Montgomeryshire Churches Survey. Church of St Melangell, Pennant Melangell*, no. 19470, 2007.

30. D. Petts, *The Early Medieval Church in Wales*, p. 128.

31. D. Petts, *The Early Medieval Church in Wales*, p. 128.

32. D. Barrington, Letter to Mr Gough, 20 July 1770, in *Illustrations of the literary history of the eighteenth century*, vol. 5 (London: Nichols, Son and Bentley, 1828), p. 583.

33. A. Tregarneth, *Founders of the Faith in Wales* (Bangor: University of Wales Press, 1996), p. 21.

34. D. Petts, *The Early Medieval Church in Wales*, pp. 177, 129.

35. Information at the site, 2014.

36. Information at the site, 2014.

Chapter Seven

1. E. Herbert McAvoy, 'Anchorites and medieval Wales', in *Anchoritic Traditions of Medieval Europe*, ed. E. Herbert McAvoy (Woodbridge: The Boydell Press, 2010), pp. 205-6.

2. '*Elucidarium* and other Tracts' p. 2, transl. T. Jones, in *The Book of the Anchorite of Llanddewi Brefi* by T. Jones, *Cardiganshire Antiquarian Society Transactions*, vol. 12, 1937, pp. 63-82.

3. E. R. Henken 'Welsh hagiography and the nationalist impulse', in *Celtic Hagiography and saints' cults*, ed. J. Cartwright (Cardiff: University of Wales Press, 2003), p. 37.

4. *Buchedd Beuno*, ch. 2, ed. and transl. A. W. Wade-Evans, *Vitae Sanctorum Britanniae et Genealogiae* (Cardiff: University of Wales Press Board, 1944).

5. O. Davies, *Celtic Christianity in Early Medieval Wales* (Cardiff, University of Wales Press, 1996), p. 18.

6. Life of Winifred, ch. 17, ed. and transl. A. W. Wade-Evans, *Vitae Sanctorum Britanniae et Genealogiae*.

7. *Buchedd Beuno*, ch. 6, ed. and transl. A. W. Wade-Evans.

8. *Buchedd Beuno*, ch. 9, ed. and transl. A. W. Wade-Evans.

9. J. G. Dunbar and I. Fisher, *Iona: A Guide to the Monuments* (Edinburgh: Her Majesty's Stationery Office, 1993), p. 15.

10. B. Stallybrass, 'Recent discoveries at Clynnogfawr', in *Archaeologia Cambrensis*, 6th series, no. 14, 1914.

11. J. R. Davies, *The Book of Llandaf and the Norman Church in Wales* (Woodbridge: The Boydell Press, 2003), p. 144.

12. Information at the site, 2014.

13. D. Gregory, *Country Churchyards in Wales*, (Llanwrst: Gwasg Carreg Gwalch, 1991), p. 76.

14. D. Petts, *The Early Medieval Church in Wales* (Stroud: The History Press, 2009), p. 102.

15. M. Thurlby, *Romanesque architecture and sculpture in Wales* (Woonton Almeley, Herefordshire: Logaston Press, 2006), p. 234.

16. Information at the site, 2014.

17. *Buchedd Beuno*, ch. 2, ed. and transl. A. W. Wade-Evans.

18. Information from a local inhabitant.

19. F. Jones, *The Holy Wells of Wales* (Cardiff: University of Wales Press, 1992), pp. 108, 179.

20. N. Edwards, 'Early Medieval Inscribed Stones and Stone Sculpture in Wales: Context and Function', in *Medieval Archaeology*, vol. 45, 2001, pp. 15-39.

21. D. Petts, *The Early Medieval Church in Wales*, pp. 42, 31.

22. Life of Winifred, ch. 17, ed. and transl. A. W. Wade-Evans.

23. T. M. Charles-Edwards, *Oxford Dictionary of National Biography* (Oxford: Oxford University Press, 2004), entry: Gwenfrewi.

24. Life of Winifred, ch. 13, ed. and transl. A. W. Wade-Evans.

25. *Buchedd Beuno*, ch. 7, ed. and transl. A. W. Wade-Evans.

26. BM Add. MS 10104, *The Chronicle of Adam of Usk (1377-1421)*, ed. and transl. C. Given-Wilson (Oxford: Clarendon Press, 1997), entry: A.D. 1416.

27. P. Caraman, ed., *The Hunted Priest: Autobiography of John Gerard* (London: Collins Fontana, 1959), p. 62.

28. C. David, *St Winefride's Well: a History and Guide* (Kildare: Leinster Leader, 1993), pp. 20, 22.

29. Information in the church, 2014.

30. Information from an older inhabitant, 24 September 2014

31. A. Chetan and D. Brueton, *The Sacred Yew* (Harmondsworth: Penguin Arkana, 1994), pp. 55, 153.

32. N. Edwards and A. Lane, 'Archaeology of the Early Church in Wales: An Introduction' in *The Early Church in Wales and the West*, ed. N. Edwards and A. Lane (Oxford: Oxbow Books, 1992), Oxbow Monograph 16, p. 9.

33. N. Edwards and A. Lane, 'Archaeology of the Early Church in Wales', pp. 9-10.

34. D. Petts, *The Early Medieval Church in Wales*, p. 104.

35. N. Edwards and T. G. Hulse, 'A Fragment of a Reliquary Casket from Gwytherin, North Wales', in *Antiquaries Journal*, vol. 72, 1994, pp. 91-101.

36. T. M. Charles-Edwards, *Oxford Dictionary of National Biography*, entry: Gwenfrewi.

37. J. and C. Bord, *Sacred Waters: Holy Wells and Water Lore in Britain and Ireland* (London: Paladin, 1986), p. 206.

Chapter Eight

1. Information at the site, 2014.

2. Information at the site, 2014.

3. Information at the site, 2014.

4. *The Dream of Maxen Wledig*, in C. Guest, transl., *The Mabinogion* (Mineola, New York: Dover Publications, 1997), pp. 52-8.

5. D. N. Dumville, ed., *The* Historia Brittonum: *The Vatican Recension* (Cambridge: D. S. Brewer, 1985), chs. 27, 29.

6. R. Bromwich, ed. and transl., *Trioedd Ynys Prydein: The Welsh Triads*, 3rd edition, (Cardiff: Cardiff University Press, 2006), pp. 441-4.

7. D. Petts, *The Early Medieval Church in Wales* (Stroud: The History Press, 2009), pp. 138, 38.

8. Bede, *The Ecclesiastical History of the English People*, ed. J. McClure and R. Collins (Oxford: Oxford University Press, 1969), bk. 2, ch. 2.

9. H. Price, 'Ecclesiastical Wealth in Early Medieval Wales', in *The Early Church in Wales and the West*, ed. N. Edwards and A. Lane (Oxford: Oxbow Books, 1992), Oxbow Monograph 16, p. 23.

10. Bede, *The Ecclesiastical History of the English People*, bk. 2, ch. 2.

11. D. N. Dumville, ed. and transl., *Annales Cambriae, A.D. 682-954: Texts A-C in Parallel* (Cambridge: Cambridge University Press, 2002), entry: A.D. 584.

12. M. Charles-Edwards, *Oxford Dictionary of National Biography* (Oxford: Oxford University Press, 2004), entry: St Deiniol.

13. D. Brook, 'The Early Christian Church East and West of Offa's Dyke', in *The Early Church in Wales and the West*, p. 100.

14. D. Brook, 'The Early Christian Church East and West of Offa's Dyke', p. 100.

15. D. Petts, *The Early Medieval Church in Wales*, pp. 42, 71.

16. L. Macinnes, *Anglesey: A Guide to the Ancient and Historic Sites on the Isle of Anglesey* (Cardiff: Cadw, Welsh Historic Monuments, 1989), p. 13.

17. L. Macinnes, *Anglesey: A Guide to the Ancient and Historic Sites*, p. 14.

18. T. Roberts, 'Welsh Ecclesiastical Place-Names and Archaeology', in *The Early Church in Wales and the West*, p. 42.

19. D. Petts, *The Early Medieval Church in Wales*, pp. 36, 130.

20. M. Redknap, 'St Davids and a new link with the Hiberno-Norse world', in *St David of Wales: Cult, Church and Nation*, Studies in Celtic History 24, ed. J. Wyn Evans and J. M. Wooding (Woodbridge: The Boydell Press, 2007), p. 86.

21. M. Redknap, 'St Davids and a new link with the Hiberno-Norse world', pp. 87-9.

22. www.museumwales.ac.uk/253; 254, accessed 18.10.2014.

23. BM Cotton MS Vespasian A xiv, composed in Cemis, Pembrokeshire.

24. D. Petts, *The Early Medieval Church in Wales*, pp. 90, 72.

25. N. Edwards and A. Lane, 'The Archaeology of the Early Church in Wales: an Introduction', in *The Early Church in Wales and the West*, p. 9.

26. R. Avent, *St Cybi's Well, Gwynedd* (Cardiff: Welsh Office, 1982), p. 3.

27. F. Jones, *The Holy Wells of Wales*, (Cardiff: University of Wales Press, 1992), p. 110.

28. F. Jones, *The Holy Wells of Wales*, p. 151.

29. A. Smyth, *Warlords and Holy Men: Scotland AD 80-1000*, 'New History of Scotland' Series (Edinburgh: Edinburgh University Press, 1984), pp. 170-71.

30. A. Tregarneth, *Founders of the Faith in Wales* (Bangor: University of Wales Press, 1996), p. 63.

31. T. Roberts, 'Welsh Ecclesiastical Place-Names and Archaeology', p. 43.

32. F. Jones, *The Holy Wells of Wales*, pp. 102, 107, 71-2.

33. E. G. Bowen, *Saints Seaways and Settlements* (Cardiff: University of Wales Press, 1969), p. 203.

34. L. Macinnes, *Anglesey: A Guide to the Ancient and Historic Sites*, p. 22.

35. L. Macinnes, *Anglesey: A Guide to the Ancient and Historic Sites*, pp. 20-24.

Chapter Nine

1. C. Knightly, *Mwynhewch Sir Ddinbych Ganoloesol* (Denbigh: Cyngor Sir Ddinbych, 1998), p. 3.

2. C. Knightly, *Mwynhewch Sir Ddinbych Ganoloesol*, p. 3.

3. H. M. R. Williams, 'The Pillar of Eliseg's Topography of Memory', paper presented at the Early Medieval Wales Archaeology Research Group (EMWARG) Conference, 2014.

4. V. Nash-Williams, *The Early Christian Monuments of Wales* (Cardiff: University of Wales Press, 1950), no. 182.

5. N. Edwards, 'Early-Medieval Inscribed Stones and Stone Sculpture in Wales: Context and Function', in *Medieval Archaeology*, vol. 45, 2001, pp. 15-39.

6. T. M. Charles-Edwards, *Wales and the Britons, 300-1064* (Oxford: Oxford University Press, 2013), pp. 449-50.

7. H. M. R. Williams, 'The Pillar of Eliseg's Topography of Memory'.

8. C. Knightly, *Mwynhewch Sir Ddinbych Ganoloesol*, pp. 3-4.

9. '*The Life of Saint David* by Rhygyfarch', ch. 2, ed. and transl. R. Sharpe and J. R. Davies in *St David of Wales: Cult, Church and Nation*, Studies in Celtic History 24, ed. J. Wyn Evans and J. M. Wooding (Woodbridge: The Boydell Press, 2007) p. 109.

10. D. R. Howlett, ed. and transl., '*Orationes Moucani*: early Cambro-Latin prayers', in *Cambridge Medieval Celtic Studies*, vol. 24, winter 1992, pp. 55-74. It is found in BL MS Royal 2A xx (saec VIII2).

11. D. E. Thornton, *Oxford Dictionary of National Biography* (Oxford: Oxford University Press, 2004), entry: Asaf.

12. 'Life of Kentigern by Jocelin of Furness', ed. and transl. A. W. Wade-Evans, *Vitae Sanctorum Britanniae et Genealogiae* (Cardiff: University of Wales Press Board, 1944), ch. 23, 188-95.

13. 'Life of Kentigern by Jocelin of Furness', ch. 23, 196-7.

14. 'Life of Kentigern by Jocelin of Furness', ch. 24, 198-200.

15. K. Jankulak, 'Alba Longa in the Celtic regions? Swine, saints and Celtic hagiography' in *Celtic Hagiography and Saints' Cults*, ed. J. Cartwright (Cardiff: University of Wales Press, 2003), pp. 272, 274.

16. 'Life of Kentigern by Jocelin of Furness', ch. 24, 203.

17. D. E. Thornton, *Oxford Dictionary of National Biography*, entry: Asaf.

18. 'Life of Kentigern by Jocelin of Furness', ch. 25, 210.

19. 'Life of Kentigern by Jocelin of Furness', ch. 25, 211-213.

20. 'Life of Kentigern by Jocelin of Furness', ch. 25, 213.

21. D. Broun, *Oxford Dictionary of National Biography*, entry: Kentigern.

22. 'Life of Kentigern by Jocelin of Furness', ch. 31, 248-9.

23. D. McRoberts, 'The death of St Kentigern of Glasgow', *Innes Review*, vol. 24, 1973, pp. 43-50.

24. 'Life of Kentigern by Jocelin of Furness', ch. 44, 343-6.

25. J. Griffiths, *A Short Guide to the Parish Church of St Asaph and St Cyndeyrn, Llanasa* (Llanasa: A5 Publications, 1986), pp. 1-2, 5.

26. D. R. Thomas, *Esgobaeth Llanelwy: A history of the diocese of St. Asaph, general, cathedral and parochial*, vol. 2, 1888, entry: Llaneurgain.

27. I am grateful to John David Evans in Llaneurgain for this information.

28. S. Baring-Gould and J. Fisher, *The Lives of the British Saints* (London: John Hodges, 1872-7), vol. 2, pp. 474, 41.

29. Information at the site, 2014.

30. Information at the site, 2014.

31. Information at the site, 2014.

32. Information at the site, 2014.

33. E. Lhuyd, *Parochalia* (1695-8), Archaeologia Cambrensis Supplement, 1909 (1910-11), p. 110.

34. B. Willis, *Survey of Bangor Cathedral* (London: Robert Gosling, 1721), p. 327.

35. R. Fenton, *Tours in Wales* (1804-13), ed. J. Fisher (London: Cambrian Archaeological Association, 1917), p. 157.

36. T. Pennant, *Tours in Wales*, ed. J. Rhys (Caernarvon: H. Humphreys, 1883), vol. 2, p. 180.

37. F. Jones, *The Holy Wells of Wales* (Cardiff: University of Wales Press, 1992), p. 173.

38. D. Petts, *The Early Medieval Church in Wales* (Stroud: The History Press, 2009), p. 191.

39. T. Roberts, 'Welsh Ecclesiastical Place-Names and Archaeology', in *The Early Church in Wales and the West*, ed. N. Edwards and A. Lane (Oxford: Oxbow Books, 1992), Oxbow Monograph 16, p. 44.

Chapter Ten

1. C. Thomas, *Celtic Britain* (London: Thames & Hudson, 1986), p. 114.

2. D. Petts, *The Early Medieval Church in Wales* (Stroud: The History Press, 2009), p. 90.

3. D. Petts, *The Early Medieval Church in Wales*, p. 90.

4. V. Nash-Williams, *The Early Christian Monuments of Wales* (Cardiff: University of Wales Press, 1950), nos. 77, 78.

5. D. Petts, *The Early Medieval Church in Wales*, pp. 116, 164.

6. E. R. Henken, 'Welsh hagiography and the nationalist impulse', in *Celtic Hagiography and saints' cults*, ed. J. Cartwright (Cardiff: University of Wales Press, 2003), p. 27.

7. Presentation at the Second Bardsey Island Spirituality Colloquium, 'Defining Enlli', organised by the Centre for the Study of Religion in Celtic Societies, Lampeter, and the Spirituality Committee of the Bardsey Island Trust, July 2005.

8. Second Bardsey Island Spirituality Colloquium.

9. P. H. Jones, *Bardsey, Its History and Wildlife* (Criccieth: Bardsey Island Trust, 1995), p. 10.

10. Second Bardsey Island Spirituality Colloquium.

11. K. Jankulak and J. M. Wooding, 'The Life of St Elgar of Ynys Enlli', in *Solitaries, Pastors and 20,000 Saints—Studies in the Religious History of Ynys Enlli (Bardsey Island)*, ed. J. M. Wooding (Lampeter: Trivium Publications, 2010).

12. K. Jankulak and J. M. Wooding, 'The Life of St Elgar of Ynys Enlli'.

13. M. Chitty, *The Monks of Ynys Enlli*, Part 1, *c.* 500 AD-1252 AD (Aberdaron: Mary Chitty, 1992), pp. 21-2.

14. From *Llawysgrif Hendreyadredd*, in O. Davies, *Celtic Spirituality*, Classics of Western Spirituality Series (New Jersey: Paulist Press, 1999), p. 278.

15. Gerald of Wales, *Journey through Wales* (1188), 2. 6. See W. Follett, *Céli Dé in Ireland: Monastic Writing and Identity in the Early Middle Ages*, Studies in Celtic History Series (Woodbridge: Boydell & Brewer, 2006), p. 3.

16. J. S. Brewer, J. F. Dimock and G. F. Warner, eds., *Giraldus Cambrensis Opera*, Rolls Series 21, 8 vols (London: 1861-91), vol. 4, p. 167.

17. K. Jankulak and J. M. Wooding, 'The Life of St Elgar of Ynys Enlli'.

18. M. Chitty, *The Monks on Ynys Enlli*, pp. 14-15.

19. K. Jankulak and J. M. Wooding, 'The Life of St Elgar of Ynys Enlli'.

20. K. Jankulak and J. M. Wooding, 'The Life of St Elgar of Ynys Enlli'.

21. *Vita Sancti Elgari*, ch. 1, transl. K. Jankukak and J. M. Wooding, in 'The Life of St Elgar of Ynys Enlli'.

22. *Vita Sancti Elgari*, ch. 2.

23. *Vita Sancti Elgari*, ch. 3.

24. *Vita Sancti Elgari*, ch. 3.

25. K. Jankulak and J. M. Wooding, 'The Life of St Elgar of Ynys Enlli'.

26. For further insight into Mother Maria's thought, see: Sr Thekla, *Mother Maria: Her life in letters* (London: Darton, Longman and Todd, 1979).

27. *Vita Sancti Elgari*, ch. 5.

28. *Vita Sancti Elgari*, ch. 5.

29. Gerald of Wales, *Descriptio Cambriae* (*Description of Wales*) (1194), bk. 2. ch. 1, transl. L. Thorpe (Harmondsworth: Penguin, 1978).

30. E. R. Henken, 'Welsh hagiography and the nationalist impulse', p. 215.

31. A. Savage and N. Watson, *Anchoretic Spirituality: Ancren Wisse and associated works*, Classics of Western Spirituality Series (New York: Paulist Press, 1991), pp. 10, 8.

32. A. Savage and N. Watson, *Anchoretic Spirituality*, pp. 7, 8.

33. Much of the research into the context of the works was carried out by J. E. Dobson, in *The Origins of Ancrene Wisse* (London: Oxford University Press, 1976), although new evidence presented by Bella Millett in 1990 challenges some of Dobson's conclusions, suggesting that the author was a Dominican friar.

34. *Ancren Wisse*, part 4 (MS Cotton Nero A.xiv), quoted in A. Savage and N. Watson, *Anchoretic Spirituality*, pp. 12, 336.

35. A. Savage and N. Watson, *Anchoretic Spirituality*, pp. 15, 44.

36. *Ancren Wisse*, Introduction, in A. Savage and N. Watson, *Anchoretic Spirituality*, p. 50.

37. *Ancren Wisse*, part 3, p. 95; see *Vitae Patrum* 7. 3, in J. P. Migne (ed.), *Patrologia Latina* (Paris, 1844-64), vol. 73, col. 1029.

38. *Ancren Wisse*, part 7, p. 189; see Cassian, *Collationes* 1, in *Patrologia Latina*, vol. 49, col. 481-90.

39. *Ancren Wisse*, part 5, pp. 164-5.

40. *Ancren Wisse*, part 5, pp. 174-5.

41. *Ancren Wisse*, part 5, p. 171.

42. *Ancren Wisse*, part 6, p. 186.

43. *Ancren Wisse*, part 8, p. 203; see Cassian, *Collationes* 24. 9, in *Patrologia Latina*, vol. 49, col. 1297-8.

44. *Ancren Wisse*, part 4, p. 132.

45. *Ancren Wisse*, part 8, p. 204.

46. *Ancren Wisse*, part 8, p. 207.

Index